The CEO Method

An Entrepreneur's Guide to Business Success

Amy Traugh

The CEO Method: An Entrepreneur's Guide to Business Success

Library of Congress Control Number: 2024902440

First edition March 2024
ISBN: 979-8-218-36020-7 (Print)
ISBN: 979-8-218-36021-4 (E-book)
Visit the author's website: amytraugh.com

To Jonathan
Thank you for believing in me
on the days when I didn't.

Free Resources to Help You on Your Entrepreneurial Journey

From the bottom of my heart, thank you for picking up this book. I'm genuinely excited to share The CEO Method with you because it's not just about making money; it's about helping you turn your aspirations into reality and create an impact.

To make your journey smoother, I've compiled some useful resources for you to use– consider them your companions as you navigate through the book.

Cheers to the journey ahead!

Resources include:

- CEO Quarterly Review Guide
- KPI Tracking Sheet
- Networking Tracker
- Business Plan Template
- And More!

Get these FREE resources by visiting **amytraugh.com/ceobook**

The CEO Method: An Entrepreneur's Guide to Business Success

Introduction

I Checked All the Boxes . . .

I have a confession to make. I am a box checker. A high-achieving, people-pleasing, type A box checker.

Graduate from college. Check.

Land my dream job. Check.

Buy a home. Check.

Marry the most amazing man I could have ever dreamed of. Check.

Have two healthy babies. Check.

I checked all the boxes and finished the "success checklist" that society conditioned me to believe would make me happy until I could retire at age 65, granted I had worked hard enough and saved enough. Then I would finally have the time and the means to do the really fun things that weren't feasible right now.

I worked so hard to check all the boxes, so why didn't I feel fulfilled? I had everything I wanted and more. Something was missing, but I couldn't quite put my finger on it.

So I did what most of us do: I accepted my current reality and started living on autopilot. Wake up, work 40 hours a week, manage the chaos of juggling parenting and work life, try to catch a breath on weekends, and take a week's vacation once a year. This endless cycle repeated itself for years until something happened to force a change.

The World Shut Down

In March of 2020, the news began buzzing with talk of a mysterious new illness emerging worldwide. It was spreading fast, and an announcement was made that, in an effort to stop the spread, schools would be shutting down for two weeks. At the time, my kiddos were in preschool and kindergarten, and without childcare, schools, or family to take care of them, we were SOL.

Fortunately, life always has a way of working out. I was offered the opportunity to take a voluntary furlough from my career in physical therapy. My family will always come first. No. Matter. What. Of course, I took advantage of this opportunity even though I was completely terrified. I'm a type A planner and this definitely wasn't part of the plan. The negative thought spiral was all-consuming, swirling in an endless cycle of what-ifs and uncertainty. This was a wake-up call that nothing in this world is ever guaranteed, including the things we so often take for granted.

Steve Jobs said, "You can't connect the dots looking forward; you can only connect them looking backwards."[1] Looking back, I can now see that was the pivotal moment when my life changed. I had spent my life checking someone else's boxes, fueled by an endless cycle of external validation that was ingrained by what have now become societal norms. I was living a mediocre life according to someone else's definition of success when I was truly meant for more. I didn't realize it at the time, but when the world shut down, my journey began because in a world where nothing was certain, anything was possible.

The Question That Changed My Life

I vividly remember the day that I realized that the life I was living was no longer aligned with what I truly wanted. It was a picture-perfect day: 72 degrees and sunny, without a cloud in the most beautiful blue sky—a rare occurrence here in Northeast Ohio. We had survived the remote-learning adventure by a thread, and finally had some room to breathe despite the ongoing uncertainty in the world around us as the pandemic continued to spread.

As our kids were outside playing, laughing, living life without a care in the world, it hit me. I was missing this. I was missing out on the time with these two amazing little humans. Cue the guilt, cue the tears, cue the anger, cue all the emotions. No matter how hard I worked or how many boxes I checked, no amount of money could ever buy back this moment in time.

1. Steve Jobs, "Words of Wisdom," commencement speech, Stanford University, Palo Alto, California, June 5,2005.

Coming to this realization was hard. So hard. What the hell was I doing? It was at that moment that I knew something had to change. I didn't know what, I didn't know how, but I knew moving forward, our lives would never be the same.

For the first time in my life, I had the opportunity to get off autopilot mode, pause, and ask myself a simple question: "What do I really want?" The answer I came up with was that I had absolutely no clue. So I dug in and confronted the deepest parts of myself that I had suppressed for so long. I acknowledged the fact that my career, the one I had worked so hard for, was no longer aligned with what I truly valued. It was at that moment that I made a decision. I made the choice to make a change by having the courage to let go of something that no longer served me.

Borrow the Belief

Flash forward four years to the time of this book's publication. I have since built multiple businesses from the ground up, completely walked away from the career I thought I would work in forever, semi-retired my husband, and most importantly, I'm finally living life on my terms. The life I had always dreamed of, yet never thought was possible for me.

It's easy to read this and think, *Wow, she's lucky.* The reality is, I am no different from you. I still have fears and doubts that creep in. I still have days where I question if going back to a 9-to-5 would be "easier." I still have old habits and perfectionist tendencies threatening to derail all the progress I have made. I have failed far more than I have succeeded.

I have cried so many times. I have been scared. I have lost friends. I have self-sabotaged. I have suffered, and still do suffer, from impostor syndrome. I am an imperfect human. I am just like you.

I wiped away the tears and learned to reframe challenges into stepping stones. I learned to be my biggest cheerleader even when no one else saw what I was doing. I chose to push through the fear and doubt. I made the choice to take messy action and show my littles that it's okay to change your mind and that failure isn't something to fear. As my friend Andrea Kaye Goodman says, "it's our willingness to go after our dreams that gives our kids permission to go after theirs." I made the choice to make a change and claim the life I had always wanted. I made the choice to let out the confident, brave, badass woman who had been hiding within me all those years so that she could make an impact on the world.

Come with Me on a Journey

I specialize in working with online service providers, but the strategies outlined in this book are applicable across most industries. This book is the exact step-by-step framework I guide clients through. It helps them to generate the money they want so they can create the impact they desire without sacrificing their two most valuable assets—time and energy. And it does this in a way that feels completely aligned with their values. But there's a catch: this process works only if you fully commit to yourself, take massive action, and push excuses to the side. If you do, you can make the life you desire a reality.

This Book Is for You If:

You are an entrepreneur who is tired of doing "all the things" and working 24-7 when nothing seems to be working.

You have an incredible product or service, but your revenue is anything short of consistent.

You are ready to stop making excuses and truly step into the CEO role of your business.

The book you hold in your hands will guide you step-by-step through my signature CEO Framework so that you can make your dreams a reality:

C: Clarity (Part One)

In Part One, we'll unpack exactly what you want your life and your business to look like.

E: Establish systems and automations (Part Two)

In Part Two, we'll give you back time and energy by establishing systems and automations that work for you.

O: Organic marketing and sales strategies (Part Three)

In Part Three, we'll dive into step-by-step strategies that will convert followers to buyers without spending money on ads.

In Part Four, we'll discuss how to take the strategies you've learned and put them into action and address the underlying mindset beliefs that may be holding you back. Spoiler alert: it's in taking action, not consuming content, that you get the results you desire.

Stepping into the role of CEO is a wild journey full of twists, turns, and unexpected surprises along the way, and I am here to be your guide as we navigate this journey together. A journey that, if you commit to taking action, WILL change your life forever.

Get ready for some tough love, a little bit of strategy, and a framework to guide you on a journey to step into your power and create a life on your terms. A life you absolutely love waking up to. A life with no regrets.

Are you ready to stop making excuses and give yourself the permission to dream bigger than you've ever dreamed before?

Then let's go! The life that you desire is waiting for you.

Part One: Clarity
Creating a Life on Your Terms

Chapter 1

What Do You Really Want?

When was the last time you asked yourself 'What do I really want?' This simple yet powerful question is one of the hardest for most people to answer, but taking the time to reflect and uncover the answer to this question is step one to designing a life on your terms. A life that's in complete alignment with your morals and your values. A life that you love waking up to every single day.

When you have a clear picture of what you want your life to look like, you can reach your destination, a.k.a. the life you desire, in a much more efficient manner, saving yourself time and energy while enjoying the journey. How is this possible? Think of life as a road trip: you need to know your destination to make any progress. If you're speeding through life without a clear idea of where you're headed, you're basically taking detours and burning fuel, resulting in wasted time and energy. Clarity is like your GPS, helping you conquer doubt by turning fear into the courage to move forward toward your destination. The longer you stay stuck in indecision because you're not sure where you're going, the more you delay reaching your goals. It's like driving in circles.

Defining your vision and values gives your journey a purpose—it's your road map for making choices that make sense for you. When you're clear about where you're headed, it's like you're creating a magnetic pull toward the future you want. Clarity activates the parts of your brain that will help you find a way to achieve your goal. It helps you kick doubts and insecurities to the curb, so you can hit the road with confidence and purpose and have the time of your life along the way.

When you gain clarity on what you really want, it's like turning on a light in a dark room. Suddenly, you can see the things that were holding you back and start clearing them out. You've got the energy to pursue your dreams now. Without that clarity, it's like you're stumbling around in the dark—you can't focus, and your efforts end up scattered. But when you intentionally focus on the actions that will move you toward your goals, you can let go of the things that don't: shiny objects like follower counts, pretty graphics, and so on. It's like decluttering your mind to save time and energy for what truly counts.

Taking the time to perform regular check-ins with yourself to assess where you are and where you are going is like hitting refresh on your goals and direction. These check-ins are your secret weapon for getting back on track when life throws you curveballs, because it will. They're not just about course correction; they're your chance to zoom out and see the big picture, especially on those days when you're ready to throw in the towel. Let's be real—we only really work for change when we can see a future that's worth the effort. It's like having this clear picture in your mind where the benefits waiting for you outweigh the challenges you'll face. It's what keeps you going, making the journey not just necessary but something you're excited about.

This Is Your Business

How many times have you found yourself caught up in the "shoulds" of your business? You know, the things you feel you should be doing just because "everyone else is doing them," like following trends, posting at certain times, and sticking to specific strategies. The result? Overwhelm sets in, and we often lose sight of what we truly want.

When you're crystal clear about how you want your business to look and feel, you reclaim the driver's seat. No more letting others dictate your every move. It's about designing a business that's authentically you.

Sure, it takes some practice, but loosening the grip on those "shoulds" and trusting your instincts? That's a game changer. So, here's a challenge: swap out the "shoulds" for "coulds" and notice the shift. Suddenly, you're back in control, making choices that genuinely feel right for you.

This is your business. Let me shout it louder for those in the back: THIS IS YOUR BUSINESS! And guess what?

YOU make the rules.

YOU get to decide how to run your business in a way that works for YOU.

YOU get to make the rules, and it doesn't matter what anyone else thinks about it.

YOU don't need to be like anyone else or do what anyone else is doing.

In this noisy world, it's easy to forget that the power to shape our lives and businesses on our terms is right within us. The lack of clarity often drags us into a whirlwind of distractions, leaving us stuck in a loop of indecision, self-doubt, and chasing after things that, deep down, don't truly resonate with us. Clarity isn't just a nice-to-have; it's the secret sauce to creating a life that feels authentic because, well, it's our life and we call the shots.

Let's pause for a moment and stop letting others define our vision for us. We've all fallen into the trap of consuming so much that our view of reality gets all twisted. It's time to clear away the noise and focus on what truly matters to us.

Now, let's have an honest conversation with ourselves. Are the goals we're chasing really ours, or are they what society told us we *should* want? With a gazillion strategies out there to reach our goals, finding the right path is like finding our own shortcut. We need a plan that works for us because, at the end of the day, we're the ones who get to choose.

Embracing the Power of the Pause

If clarity is key, how do we begin to uncover what we truly want? Many of us live our lives on autopilot and, for many of us, pausing is extremely uncomfortable and feels counterproductive. We are forced to confront parts of ourselves that we've suppressed for years or even decades, including deep-rooted beliefs that we have created our identity around. We've glamorized the hustle, become addicted to the constant noise, and worn "busy" like a badge of honor because we have been conditioned to think that more hustle will yield more success. So, we cling to the hustle, fearing that if we pause for a moment, we might fall behind.

Evolution into the version of ourselves that we truly desire to be involves letting go of our old identity, which brings up subconscious fears. We uncover feelings that suggest we're not really as happy as the smile we wear in the filtered images that we're hiding behind on social media because we've allowed the opinions of others to be more valuable than our own.

It's in the hustle that we are constantly trying to prove our worth. How many jobs incentivize productivity and the ability to multitask? Heck, I came from a career where productivity was factored into our merit raises.

Multitasking is one of the biggest lies we have been sold as a society. When we are trying to do everything for everyone, we end up losing our focus and accomplishing far less than we would have if we'd channeled that energy to focus on one task at a time. Identify your priorities and schedule these on your calendar first, so you can refocus your time and energy by prioritizing what really matters to you and will create the results you desire.

The constant hustle is not a fast track to success; rather, it's a fast track to burnout. We are human beings, not human doings, and there is power in the pause. It's impossible to grow unless you know where you are, and slowing down is often the fastest way of speeding up your results.

Does Technology Control You?

This may seem like a strange question, but do you control technology or does technology control you? How often throughout the day are you beckoned by the ding of your phone? An alert of a new email? Maybe a Facebook or Instagram notification that someone has messaged you? Do you find yourself filling your downtime consuming information and staring at the screen of a device you hold in your hand? The average American touches their phone upward of 2,617 times each day and spends upward of 2 hours and 30 minutes on their phone.[2]

In order to truly figure out exactly what you want, you must quiet the external noise all around you by decreasing your consumption so you can tune into your inner voice. All the answers you are searching so hard for are within. The key is eliminating distractions so that you can focus on the task at hand versus task switching. A simple way to do this is through an exercise I call a tech detox. This simple exercise sounds easy, but prepare yourself for a challenge!

---

2. Michael Winnick, "Putting a Finger on Our Phone Obsession," *dscout,* July 16, 2016, http://tinyurl.com/3cd6k9xz.

Notifications

The first thing I want you to do is to open the settings on your phone and remove all of the notifications. If you do a significant amount of work from your phone, place the apps you use for work on a separate screen or in a separate folder and remove any non-essential apps so you aren't tempted to catch up on "just a few things" from time to time.

What you will quickly notice is how often you habitually pick up your phone when you hear or see a notification pop up, thereby pulling focus away from the task at hand. Moving the apps from the home screen will require more effort to access the app, bringing your action into intentional awareness. This awareness can be helpful in refocusing your attention.

According to a study by the University of California, Irvine, it can take upward of 23 minutes on average to return to the original task at hand following a distraction.[3] That's insane! Think about what you could accomplish in 23 minutes. Multiply the number of distractions you are faced with at any given time and it's incredible that anything gets accomplished.

Email

Email is another source of distraction for many of my clients. Schedule times throughout your workday to check your email instead of keeping it open in the background while you work. The vast majority of us are not working under life-and-

3. Gloria Mark, "The Cost of Interrupted Work: More Speed and Stress" (Irvine, CA: March 2015) https://ics.uci.edu/~gmark/chi08-mark.pdf.

death circumstances and, therefore, we do not need to reply instantly to our emails. If this really bothers you, turn on an email auto-reply and state a clear time frame within which your recipient can expect a response.

Social Media

For many of us, spending time on social media is a part of our daily routine. Simply setting an intention and time limit for yourself each time you use social media can save you hours of time. Is your intent to make a post? Is it to nurture relationships with prospective clients? Is it to reply to comments and build community? It's easy to get caught up scrolling your feed because the algorithm is designed to pique your interest and keep you on the platform. What ends up happening is your brain tricks you into thinking that because you're scrolling, you're doing something. Well, yes, you are technically doing something; however, that something often results in wasting your valuable time and energy. Scrolling social media for inspiration can actually decrease your creativity, which in turn makes you blend in with all the noise.

In a Creative Slump?

Here are some things you can do when you're in a creative slump instead of scrolling for inspiration.

- Unplug and take a break.
- Take a walk, exercise, or move your body.
- Read a book.
- Do something to pamper yourself.

- Repurpose a piece of old content.
- Practice meditation or breath work.
- Do something fun or something that brings you joy.
- Talk with a friend.
- Journal.
- Listen to music.
- Write a thank-you note.

Have you noticed a theme with the tech detox? It comes down to making the choice to be intentional about how you spend your time. When you are intentional, you focus on the tasks that will get you the results that you desire. When you get the results you desire, you begin to make the life you dream of a reality.

What Is Your Why?

When you have taken the time to identify exactly what you want and where you are going, it's extremely important to know exactly why you want the things you say you desire. The what and the how are always confusing until you get clear on the why. Think of your rooted why as your guiding light, your North Star, that guides you toward your destination. When you know why, the how will come. All of the hows will be meaningless unless your why is strong enough. When your why is clear and deeply rooted, your commitment to it will be more powerful than the excuses and challenges life will throw your way.

Often, buried deep down, we know exactly what we want, but we give up quickly when life gets hard because we're relying on fleeting motivation to reach our goals. More often than not, the only thing standing between you and the life you desire is, well . . . you. And that's a tough pill to swallow.

When your why is bigger than your excuses, you learn to trust yourself and break the cycle of external validation and people-pleasing because you have given yourself permission to create the life that you crave. You can take steps to regain control and live a life on your own terms and release those things that have been holding you back and no longer serve you.

As a business owner, there will be challenges, obstacles, and detours along the way. Your why will get you through the challenging times when you are tempted to quit and on the days when no one sees the work you're putting in to grow your business. If you stay committed, imagine how different your life will look one month from now, or six months, or a year.

When you pause and unpack not only exactly what it is that you truly want, but why you want it, you have something that you can intentionally work toward and can make a plan to help you get there in the most efficient way possible. You start to embrace the beautiful journey that's been flying by you, the one you've been too busy to notice.

This is your life and your business, and you get to choose how you want it to look. When you take the time to uncover what you truly want and why you want it, you reclaim your power and begin to design the life that you want. You only get one shot at life, and you owe yourself the permission to create the life and legacy you desire. Go out and make it happen!

Action Item: Uncovering Your Why

Joe Stumpf developed a simple yet powerful exercise called "Seven Levels Deep."[4] This exercise will help you identify the root of your why.

Ask yourself:

- What is it that you truly desire?
    - Why is it important for you to (your answer)?
        - Why is it important for you to (insert your previous answer)?

Continue asking yourself this same question until you get to the seventh level to truly unpack why it is important to you to become successful. This may take some deep reflection. However, unpacking exactly what you want and why you want it is the key to unlocking your deeper purpose.

---

4. Joe Stumpf, "Joe Stumpf demonstrates the 5-6-7 exercise," *By Referral Only,* September 30, 2011, YouTube video, 13:39, https://youtu.be/kbepE_r8aO0?feature=shared.

Chapter 2

Living a Life on Your Terms

How do you expect to get what you want when you don't know what it is that you want?

Now that you have taken the time to intentionally turn down the noise around you, have you noticed those thoughts playing on repeat in your head? It's like your mind has its own playlist. Regaining control and living a life on your terms begins with awareness. This awareness equips you with the ability to acknowledge these thoughts, rewrite the stories that no longer serve you, and release the beliefs keeping you in your current reality — the reality that you previously couldn't see beyond.

Awareness of your thoughts will ensure your actions and words are aligned with what you desire because when you are focused on the past, you are blind to the present. Having doubts is completely normal; it's your brain's way of being a little overprotective because it's trying to keep you safe. However, letting your doubts stop you is a choice that you get to make.

As you dive into your thoughts, don't shy away from those emotions that start bubbling up. It's that tricky point where many of us hit a roadblock—dealing with feelings of guilt, frustration, and sadness can be a real challenge. Don't dodge those emotions. If you ever feel stuck, there are plenty of amazing resources and people out there ready to support you on your journey.

I challenge you to let go of where you thought you would be by now and take a moment to get quiet and accept and acknowledge exactly where you are in this very moment. It's like giving your internal GPS your starting point, which is essential to finding the most efficient route to your destination. To hit your goals, you've got to pause, pinpoint where you are, and tweak your actions accordingly.

It is your responsibility to take the time to get clear on exactly what you want your life to look like. Your life is your responsibility, and no one else is responsible for creating the life you live but you.

The Questions That Will Change Your Life

I encourage you to block out time on your schedule and actually write down your answers to the following questions. Why writing? Writing makes your brain pay attention. This process doesn't have to be done all at once, and I must warn you that it may get uncomfortable. The life-changing clarity you need is just past the temporary discomfort of answering these questions. When you get clear on exactly what you want, you can take action to go after it. The key is to get honest with yourself so you can live the life you truly desire. Grab a notebook and your favorite drink and let's dig in.

Identifying Where You Are Right Now:

- How do I feel?

- How's my physical health?

- Am I getting enough sleep?

- Am I exercising on a regular basis?

- How am I eating?

- How's my mental health?

- What keeps me up at night?

- How do I view myself?

- What fears are holding me back right now?

- Are these fears valid?

- What is going well for me and giving me energy, joy, and satisfaction?

- What's working?

- What motivates me?

- What is my biggest strength?

- What have been some of my recent wins?

- What isn't feeling good in my life and is draining my energy?

- What isn't working?

- Where am I playing small?

- What obstacles and challenges am I facing?

- What happens if I ignore these challenges?

- Why haven't I achieved my goals yet?

- Am I waiting to take action on the things that would move me closer to my goals?

- What's holding me back from asking for what I need or want?

- What am I doing?

- How am I spending my time?

- What does my current schedule look like?

- Am I prioritizing the things that are important to me?

- Am I maintaining my boundaries?

- Do my actions align with my goals?

- Am I disciplined and holding myself accountable for my actions?

- How am I showing up every day, even on the hard ones?

- Who am I surrounded by?

- What season of life am I in?

- What am I doing for fun?

- What habits do I currently have that don't support my goals?

- What do I truly want?

- What am I trying to accomplish?

- How will achieving the goals I want improve my life?

- What matters most to me?

- Am I doing anything because I think I should?

Identifying Where You Want to Be:

- If I were to wake up tomorrow having achieved all of the goals that I have set, what would my life look like?

- How do I feel?

- How's my physical health?

- Am I getting enough sleep?

- Am I exercising on a regular basis?

- How am I eating?

- How's my mental health?

- How do I view myself?

- What have I let go of?

- What do I no longer tolerate?

- What is going well for me and giving me energy, joy, and satisfaction?

- Where am I?

- What's working?

- What motivates me?

- What have some of my recent wins been?

- What am I doing?

- How am I spending my time?

- What does my ideal day look like?

- How does every day feel?

- What am I doing more of?

- What am I doing less of?

- Am I maintaining my boundaries?

- What am I doing for fun?

- How am I showing up because I have what I want?

- What are my priorities and daily nonnegotiables?

- How do I show up when times get hard?

- How do I handle challenges?

- Who am I surrounded by?

- How do I act and carry myself?

- What habits have I changed to support the life I desire?

Bridging the Gap

Now that you have taken the time to identify where you are and where you want to be, we can bridge the gap by uncovering who you need to become and what you need to do in order to create the reality you desire.

- What would it take to achieve my goals, and what am I willing to do to get there?

- How will achieving this make me feel?

- If I knew I couldn't fail, what would I do differently?

- What does success look like to me?

- What am I afraid of as I think about achieving my goals?

- What needs to change?

- What is standing in the way of achieving my goals?

- What is holding me back from taking action?

- What would I go after if I knew I would definitely achieve it?

- Am I investing my time in resources which will help me achieve the results I desire?

- Am I surrounding myself with people who will help me achieve the results I desire?

- What do I need to start doing to get myself closer to my goal?

- What do I need to stop doing that no longer serves me?

- What am I no longer available for?

- How can I stay accountable?

- If nothing changes, what happens?

- How do I need to show up?

- Am I willing to stretch out of my comfort zone and take risks?

- Am I operating as the person my dreams require?

- What can I do to show up as my future self today?

- How would I show up if I had a line out the door of people wanting my product or service?

- What beliefs do I need to embody?

- If I had more time, how would I be spending it?

- How will I know when I've achieved the success I desire? Create a list: "I know I'll be successful when . . . "

When you have clarity on exactly where you are and what you want, you can unpack exactly who you need to become and what actions you need to take in order to get the results you want.

Focusing on the Who Versus the How

Our thoughts and feelings are like the storytellers of our beliefs, shaping whether we dive into action or get stuck in the land of excuses. When you foster the inner belief that the life you dream of is actually doable, it's like opening a door to a room full of fresh opportunities. Those opportunities? They're like stepping stones, creating a path forward and leading you straight to your goals.

This creates momentum and momentum creates results. You experience what you believe, therefore changing your beliefs is like unlocking a secret door to the results you're hungry for. Change only kicks in when the pain of staying put outweighs the discomfort of making a shift. All too often, we're spending more time avoiding the things that cause us pain versus confronting the underlying issues.

Picture your brain as a detective constantly looking for clues to confirm what you already believe. This is why it is so important to truly embody the person you desire to become. Show up as her every day because your brain will search for evidence proving your new identity and will filter out anything that challenges these beliefs. Identifying and tackling your limiting beliefs head-on is like preparing for battle. You're arming yourself to handle the challenges that will pop up. It's a way to show your brain that your goals are not just dreams but real, achievable things. Life doesn't get better by chance; it gets better by intentional change. The power is in your hands, so make the choice to make a change if you aren't satisfied with where you are.

The trajectory of your life is up to you, and the person you want to become is already within you, waiting for you to reach your full potential. Instead of getting bogged down by the "how," try shifting your focus to the "who." Who do I need to become to get the results I desire? When you embody the version of yourself that you want to be, things change. You show up differently, you carry yourself differently, and before you know it, those subconscious, self-sabotaging habits start fading away. It's like this cool, behind-the-scenes transformation that sets you on a path to create the impact you were born to make on this world.

Anna Delvey, though definitely not a good role model, provides us with a great example of truly embodying the person you desire to be. She posed as a wealthy German heiress and conned hundreds of thousands of dollars out of banks, friends, and acquaintances without a dime to her name. She almost succeeded in purchasing a building on Park Avenue in New York City prior to her arrest and subsequent conviction. How did she pull it off? Anna's unwavering belief in her own identity was the key. Her self-assurance was so powerful that it convinced others to believe in the persona she projected.

Confidence is the cornerstone of sales—it begins with selling yourself. If you don't believe in yourself and what you're offering, how can others trust you to solve their problems? Your first sale must be to yourself. This inner belief is pivotal; it propels your ability to resonate with potential clients, creating an aura that establishes trust. Confidence, in essence, lies in your ability to engage, understand, and provide solutions. It's an attribute that draws people toward you.

At its core, confidence is having the courage to start before you feel ready, a by-product of consistent action despite fear, which builds a foundation of self-trust. When obstacles arise, confident individuals take responsibility, demonstrating unwavering commitment to themselves and their desired outcomes.

Confidence is not a passive trait; it's a learned skill. Waiting until you feel confident is a delaying tactic. Instead, practice becomes the path to self-trust. We lack confidence because we're lacking certainty in what the future holds, which makes us fear the unknown. You have to be willing to do what most people won't to get the results that most people don't. You can't be disappointed in the results you didn't get from the work you didn't do. When you're playing small, you're denying yourself the opportunity to impact others.

Visualization

Visualization is a powerful tool that gives your brain a sneak peek into the life you want. It's not just a mental exercise; it's your brain's way of gearing up for the journey ahead. It's a bit like a rehearsal before the big show because our brain lacks the ability to distinguish between thinking about doing something and actually doing it. By spending some quality time visualizing your goals, you're sending a clear message to your brain that this is really important to you. And you know what happens next? You find yourself naturally leaning into actions that align with those dreams. It's like giving your brain a road map to follow, making your desires more tangible and achievable. This powerful technique is backed by extensive research and is frequently utilized by professional athletes, speakers, and entertainers to enhance their performance.

Action Item: Daily Visualization

Take a few deep breaths, and think of a specific moment in your past when you experienced a huge success, accomplishment, or win. Allow yourself to relive this experience, picturing every detail around you and feeling the emotion that was present in that moment. Now, envision in vivid detail the life that you desire. What does it look like? Who is surrounding you? How do you feel? Picture yourself taking the actions that would create the results you want. Channel this feeling and repeat this exercise daily to create proof to your brain that you are capable of taking the actions needed to get the outcome you desire. Show your brain that you are willing to do the things that scare you despite the fear currently holding you back.

Chapter 3

Gaining Clarity in Your Business

After you have taken the time to figure out exactly what you want your life to look like, it's time to establish a business that will support the life you desire. Just as you took stock of your life, it's important to assess where you are and where you want to be. This allows you to reverse engineer your goals and create a plan to achieve the results you want.

Your Business Snapshot

Review the current state of your business by asking yourself the following questions:

- Why does my business exist?

- What are the mission, vision, and values of my business?

- What do I stand for?

- What makes me different from others in my industry and the best choice?

- Why should someone work with me?

- How do I want my clients to feel?

- What's working well right now?

- What challenges am I experiencing in the business?

- What is my current business net profit or net loss?

- What is my current business overhead?

- What other expenses do I have?

- What is my current profit margin?

- What's selling and what's not selling?

- What was my top-grossing product or service?

- What offers do I currently have?

- What is my income goal?

- What are my monthly and yearly income targets?

- Do I want my business to be my primary source of income?

- Do my current products and offers support my goals?

- What is my time capacity, and what is my maximum income potential at my current capacity?

- How many client-facing hours do I need to accomplish my goals?

- How many hours am I spending on the back-end tasks in my business?

- Do I need to outsource anything in order to create more time so that I can focus on client-facing activities and achieve my goals without burnout?

- How many hours am I working each week?

- How many hours do I want to be working each week?

- If I took money off the table, what would my next move be?

- What am I investing in?

- What investments would move my business forward?

- Who do I enjoy working with?

- What are the shared attributes of these clients?

- Are my current leads qualified?

Identifying Your Ideal Client

Clarity as to the problem you solve and who you solve it for will allow you to create content that positions your business as the perfect solution for your ideal clients. Keep your messaging clear, not clever, because clever messaging often creates confused customers who are less likely to hit that Buy button.

- What is the specific problem you solve for your ideal client?

- What are you the go-to for?

- What is the transformation you provide?

- How do you solve the problem they have and create the transformation they desire?

- Why do they need to solve this problem?

- What impact do their current problems have on their lives?

- How will solving this problem help them and make their life easier?

- Will it save them time, energy, or money?

- Will it improve their health or other aspects of their life?

- What are the consequences if they don't solve their problem?

- What are they going through right now?

- Who do you solve this problem for?

- What are your ideal clients' challenges and struggles?

- What keeps them up at night?

- What are their fears?

- What are their past experiences with the product or service you provide?

- What thoughts, excuses, beliefs, and behaviors are holding them back or keeping them stuck?

- What is the root cause of their problems?

- What are they avoiding doing that would get them results?

- What are your ideal clients' goals and desires?

- How do they want to feel?

- What are their values and beliefs?

- What motivates them?

- What do they say they want?

- What do they actually need? Why?

- Why do they need it?

- What do they need next?

- What do they need to start doing?

- What do they need to stop doing?

- Are they aware they have a problem?

- Are they aware you have the solution to the problem they have?

- Why haven't they achieved their goals yet?

- Why do they need you to get them there?

- How are you the solution to the problem they have?

- Are they ready to buy?

- Why now?

- What motivates your buyers to spend money on the solution?

- Can they afford your solution?

- Do they have the ability to make the decision to buy?

- Do they see the value and benefits of your solution?

- What objections do they have?

- What are the misconceptions they have about your product or service?

- Where are your ideal clients?

- Are they local or online? What online platforms do they use?

- How are they consuming information?

- How are your current clients finding you?

- How are you positioning yourself in front of your ideal client?

- How are you bringing people into your world daily?

- How can you connect with more of your ideal clients and grow your community?

Power of One

Unpacking the answers to these questions can take some work and may require market research. Once you're crystal clear on that one product or service that solves a specific problem for a particular person, you position yourself as their go-to solution. It might sound a bit surprising, but even the giants started small by focusing on just one thing. Think Nike—they kicked off with running shoes. Starbucks? They started by perfecting coffee. Amazon? It all began with books. So, embracing simplicity and clarity in what you offer? That's your ticket to building something remarkable.

It's easy to get caught up in the cycle of chasing shiny objects, thinking you need a bit of everything to make it work. Podcasts, memberships, micro-offers, group programs, one-on-one sessions—the list never ends. But here's the inside scoop: take a breath and map out your offers. What's your freebie? What's the wallet-friendly option? And what's the big-ticket magic? It's so tempting to glance at what everyone else is up to, but until you've got that one product or service raking in consistent sales, hold off on adding more to your plate.

In summary, working through this takes time, but it's time well spent because lack of clarity is what holds business owners back from getting the results they desire. Awareness is the first step to change. When you have absolute clarity as to what exactly you want, why you want it, and who you need to be to make it happen, you will be able to design a business you love. You'll build it on your terms, in a way that feels aligned to your goals and desires, and in a way that saves you time and energy.

Action Item: Gain Clarity

Take the time to answer the questions outlined in this chapter to gain clarity. We will use this information in Part Three.

Part Two: Establish Systems and Automations toRegain Control of Your Time and Energy

Chapter 4

Stepping into the Role of CEO

True CEOs are the visionaries and leaders of their companies. In order to truly step into the role of CEO, you need to skillfully manage your two most valuable assets—your time and your energy. All too often, entrepreneurs get caught in the whirlwind of constant work, juggling tasks in the pursuit of flexibility and freedom. Yet, here's the harsh truth: an addiction to the hustle is a fast track to burnout.

So, how do you reclaim control over your time? Brace yourself because I have bad news for you—you won't find the time; you have to make it by prioritizing what truly matters to you. The key? Be intentional about how you spend your time and where you direct your focus in the precious time you have available.

Time Audit

Ever feel like time has slipped away, and you're left wondering where it went? In order to have freedom of time, you need to take ownership of your schedule. That's where the magic of a time audit comes in—a simple yet eye-opening exercise that will help you identify how you are spending your time.

Pick a day, or better yet, three, and jot down every little thing you do in real time. Everything from scrolling through socials to diving into emails, taking calls, working with clients, and tackling those behind-the-scenes tasks. Hint: most phones now track app usage, so you can get a sneak peek into your time habits. It's like shining a light on where your precious minutes really go. Be specific in your documentation and list tasks like checking emails or content creation versus "working."

After you have taken the time to document your day, it's time to analyze the data. Your schedule is a direct reflection of your priorities and what you are committed to. Look for activities that consume a significant amount of time but don't contribute much to your goals. These are potential time wasters that you may need to address. Evaluate your productivity during specific times of the day. Identify when you are most focused and when your energy tends to dip. This insight can help you optimize your schedule. Based on your analysis, determine your priorities. Allocate more time to activities that align with your goals and contribute to your well-being.

By conducting a thorough time audit, you gain a clear understanding of how you spend your time, enabling you to make intentional choices that align with your priorities and objectives. It uncovers those sneaky moments when time slips away and allows you to identify opportunities to work smarter. All too often as entrepreneurs, we end up doing things to make ourselves feel busy when in reality these aren't income-producing activities (IPAs). As you pinpoint these distractions, you discover hidden pockets of time you never thought you had, allowing you to zero in on those needle-moving IPAs. Almost always, it's not about lacking time; it's about putting focus on what truly moves the needle toward your goals and saying no to distractions.

When Motivation Fades

Most of us like to consider ourselves perpetually motivated, myself included—heck, it's in the title of my podcast, The Motivated CEO. While it's true that motivation is often a catalyst to create action, things beyond your control will happen and the motivation you felt when first starting out will fade. This is where it gets hard. Life happens, tragedy happens, illness happens, circumstances seemingly out of our control happen. When obstacles appear, it's easy to revert to what is safe and familiar. In times of uncertainty, when you don't have control over the circumstances around you, remember that even though you can't necessarily control the event, you can control how you respond. What can you learn from this? How can you use this unfortunate circumstance as a gift to help you grow? The key is to not let these events derail you; rather, use them as opportunities to grow and become even more resilient.

So, how do you continue to make progress on days the motivation fades and you don't feel like showing up? The secret is commitment. Making a commitment to yourself and taking responsibility for your thoughts, beliefs, actions, focus, and energy. The more disciplined you become, the quicker you shift from negotiating with your own mind to taking unwavering actions that pave the way for the results you crave. Action creates momentum and momentum creates results.

When I worked in my 9-to-5, there were plenty of days when I would have rather stayed in bed because I was tired and didn't feel motivated, but I knew that in order to keep my job, I had to remain disciplined and hold myself accountable by keeping the promises I had made to myself and others.

Commitment to yourself has a compound effect. We often think it's the big moves that yield massive results in our businesses, but truth be told, it's the unwavering discipline with the small day-to-day actions that truly shapes our outcomes. It's all the little things you do to show up even when no one seems to be watching. After all, if you can't commit to the small things, how do you expect to navigate the resistance that inevitably comes with the big challenges?

When there's a lack of commitment, our excuses become stronger than our dreams. It's up to you to make the decision to take action to achieve the results that you desire. It doesn't matter where you came from; what matters is where you are now and where you want to go, and commitment will get you there faster. Making a decision gets you into action because you will never build a successful business with just intentions and plans.

Take accountability for your actions or lack thereof and stop the victim mentality. When you make a mistake, learn from it and own it. Don't blame someone else when the only person you should really blame is the person staring back at you in the mirror. When you start showing up and acting like the person you want to become, you are changing how you are viewed by your subconscious. Commitment to yourself and the outcome you want is key. There will always be disappointments, setbacks, and surprises along the way. Your level of commitment and persistence during the tough times is a direct measure of your belief in yourself. Achieving your goals or not often comes down to whether you are willing to make the commitment and take the necessary actions by getting out of your own way.

Your life is your responsibility. There will never be a right time, and you will never feel ready. At the end of the day, you need to remain committed to your vision of the life you want to live and hold yourself accountable. You have to put in the work because it's what you do today that creates tomorrow's results.

One day, you will look back and thank yourself for remaining committed. The question is are you willing to stay committed and make the sacrifices needed to be successful in your life?

Establish Your Daily Nonnegotiables

Establishing a list of daily nonnegotiables will help you stay disciplined and keep your business moving forward on the tough days. Daily nonnegotiables are essential because once time is spent, you cannot get it back.

Here's an overview of my daily nonnegotiables. Feel free to use them to get started with identifying your own daily nonnegotiables.

N: Network

O: Outbound lead generation

N: Nurture

Network

If you're an introvert like me, the mere thought of networking may trigger a heart-racing, cold-sweat reaction. I still remember the first networking event I attended. As everyone flawlessly introduced themselves, I sat there, armpits sweating excessively, my heart palpitating, and fought the feeling that I was going to pass out. When it was time for me to introduce myself, I'm not sure if I articulated a coherent statement. The best part about this networking event? It was online.

Flash forward a few years and I genuinely love networking. I've pushed past the discomfort, redefined my approach, and now see networking as a chance to build meaningful connections. If you're still unsure about making this strategy work for you, remember this—people love to talk about themselves. By asking thoughtful questions, you uncover common ground, get to know them better, and build authentic, deep connections.

Expanding your network isn't just about widening the circle; it's about unlocking a world of collaborative possibilities with like-minded individuals. Shifting your networking mindset from a sales-centric approach to one rooted in service is the key to unlocking even more doors—specifically those leading to potential referral partners. You don't have the capacity to serve every client to the extent they may need, therefore having an extensive network of trusted providers becomes your secret weapon. This not only allows you to stay true to your zone of genius but also empowers you to better serve your clients by seamlessly connecting them with the expertise they need. It's not just networking; it's building a dynamic ecosystem of collaboration and mutual support.

Anything you need to succeed in business is literally an ask away. The person you are connecting with may not have the solution you are looking for or the resources you need available, but they most likely can connect you with someone who does. The inverse is true too. The person you are speaking with may not need what you have to offer, but they may know someone who does. You never know who will bring up your name in a room, even when you're not actually present. This is the power of relationship capital. By simply being human, seeking to serve and to build relationships with others, you remain top of mind.

One of my go-to questions during networking is "What do you need help with right now?" This straightforward question effortlessly cuts through surface-level conversation, leaving a lasting impression. It signals a genuine interest in the other person's journey, challenges, and growth. This approach not only fosters collaboration but also builds trust, increasing the likelihood that the connection will evolve into a meaningful relationship beyond the initial networking encounter.

By expressing a sincere willingness to help, you set the stage for a reciprocal exchange. This openness often inspires the other person to inquire about your needs or offer their assistance in return, creating the opportunity for a mutually beneficial and enduring relationship.

Outbound Lead Generation

Lead generation serves as the foundation, laying the groundwork for increased visibility of your product or service. It's a pivotal initial phase, setting the stage for transforming followers into buyers, a topic we'll explore more extensively in Part Three. The primary objective of outbound lead generation isn't immediate sales. The goal is to strategically position yourself in front of your ideal clients, provide massive value, and then present a solution to the challenges they face.

Nurture

In the fast-paced world of entrepreneurship, it's easy to get caught up in the allure of follower counts and vanity metrics. Sure, they provide validation, but let's take a moment to reflect—when was the last time you were genuinely of service to those in your world? Consider this: when someone eagerly opts in to your email list, enticed by a freebie or resource, do you go beyond the transaction to consistently offer them more value? How about those new social media followers—do you take a moment to say hello and actively engage with them?

Shift your focus toward going above and beyond for your existing clients, reaching out to past clients and referral partners, and having genuine conversations with those already following you. Successful selling is all about building relationships and fostering the essential elements of "know, like, and trust." These three keys are vital to creating a strong connection with your audience and, ultimately, driving sales.

As the CEO of your business, it's easy to cut yourself some slack when others aren't there to hold you accountable. Ultimately, it's up to you to stay disciplined so you obtain the results you desire. Taking the time to pinpoint your daily nonnegotiable activities is a strategic move that allows you to redirect your precious time, especially on challenging days when motivation fades. This ensures that every moment is purposefully directed toward the growth of your business.

Action Item: Daily Nonnegotiables

What are your daily nonnegotiables? Write them down in a place where you will see them daily to hold yourself accountable.

Chapter 5

The Best System Available

If you perform a search for the best business systems online, your search will generate billions of results. We are at the height of a technology boom that doesn't appear to be slowing down anytime soon, especially as artificial intelligence (AI) tools get more and more sophisticated. Navigating the endless options available can make the task of choosing the right one feel like quite a monumental feat. Especially when you're just starting out, resist the temptation to dive into complex platforms with endless fancy bells and whistles that come with a hefty monthly price tag. The best system is the system that works best for you.

Your ideal system isn't about perfection; it's about aligning with your workflow and functionality. Simple often triumphs over complex. Take the time to pinpoint areas where a system can streamline your operations by eliminating unnecessary tasks. I've discovered that simplicity tends to succeed more frequently than intricate setups. Systems create structure and structure creates freedom. They enable you to identify tasks that can be easily outsourced or delegated, especially those with a low return on investment (ROI). Offloading such tasks not only saves you time but also contributes to significant cost savings.

Focused Effort

In my 16 years as an outpatient clinician, I adhered to a schedule, treating patients every 30 minutes for 11 hours a day or more. The clinic setting provided a structured framework; each day unfolded predictably. I would walk into the clinic and perform treatment after treatment, mapped out per my schedule, until the day was over. I was used to having a rigid structure telling me exactly what to do and when to do it.

Transitioning into entrepreneurship, I realized the need to leverage what had worked for me in the past. For the initial six months of running my business, I had to adopt a schedule broken down into 30-minute intervals in order to stay on task. I am by no means implying that this is the strategy that you should take. I share this with you to illustrate the importance of identifying how you work best. Leverage your knowledge of what works best for you to run your business in a way that will give you back control of your time and energy.

The beautiful part of running a business is the inherent flexibility. Harness this flexibility to your advantage. When are you most productive? Do you find your energy peaks in the morning, or do you function better later in the day? Remember, it's your business, and you have the authority to organize your time in a way that works for you. There are various methods available: time blocking, the Pomodoro Technique, task batching, and more. Experiment with different approaches to find a technique that works best for you.

Implementing a System

The thought of diving into systems might be a bit overwhelming, but it's crucial to recognize that systems are designed to alleviate your workload by streamlining processes. As your business grows, you'll inevitably reach a point of capacity, and that's where the beauty of structure comes into play, offering you freedom. Systems become your ally in reclaiming time and energy by introducing order and eliminating unnecessary tasks from your schedule—tasks that might currently be vying for your attention but aren't essential. Systems and structures allow you to repeat results, thereby creating freedom.

Before you consider investing in an expensive system with features you may never use, I encourage you to start by mapping out your standard operating procedures (SOP). An SOP is essentially a step-by-step guide outlining the actions required to achieve a specific outcome. Throughout the week, take the time to list all your offers and business tasks. Consider using tools like Loom or other screen recording platforms to document yourself performing different activities. This way, when the time comes to outsource, you'll have a comprehensive process documented from start to finish, making it easier to teach someone else without additional effort on your part.

Take your email strategy, for instance. What's your process for sending out emails? Is there a specific pattern for certain days? How do you schedule them? Where do you source the graphics for your emails? If you have a podcast, what's the workflow from recording to publication? Similarly, outline your client-onboarding process—from securing the contract and receiving payment to delivering the service they've paid for. Map out each task and offer, step by step, to create a clear road map for your business processes.

Automations

If you find yourself stuck in the loop of repetitive tasks, there's likely an automation solution waiting for you. With technology advancing at an unprecedented pace, the specific automation options may vary. Many email platforms, for example, come equipped with built-in automations ready to effortlessly send out your deliverables automatically when a warm lead opts into your offer. Set it up once, and it seamlessly boosts efficiency without requiring your ongoing involvement.

While I won't go into specific automations here, platforms like YouTube provide a wealth of step-by-step tutorials, guiding you on implementing tailored automations for your business needs.

Taking the time to map out your processes not only grants you a clear understanding of your workflow but also allows you to identify opportunities for automation. Utilizing technology to handle back-end tasks not only enhances efficiency but also significantly lightens your workload. It's a strategic move that frees up your time, allowing you to focus on the aspects of your business that truly demand your attention and creativity. In essence, automations empower business owners to work smarter, not harder. They contribute to increased productivity, improved customer satisfaction, and the overall success and sustainability of the business.

Decision Fatigue

In the course of a day, we find ourselves making countless decisions, ranging from the mundane, like choosing what to have for breakfast, to decisions which require higher level reasoning such as building out a new offer. The sheer volume of decisions we encounter can lead to what experts term "decision fatigue." As we navigate through these choices, the quality of our decision-making ability tends to diminish. This is where the power of SOPs becomes evident. SOPs act as invaluable guides, alleviating decision fatigue by offloading routine information from our minds. By doing so, we conserve precious mental energy, allowing us to channel our focus and creativity into decisions that truly drive our business forward.

SOPs provide a clear road map for routine tasks. By documenting and standardizing processes, business owners and their teams don't have to grapple with recurring decisions. The established procedures act as a reliable guide, ensuring a consistent and streamlined approach to daily operations. This clarity minimizes the mental strain associated with making repetitive decisions, freeing up cognitive resources for more strategic thinking.

SOPs act as a powerful antidote to decision fatigue by providing structure and guidance. By transforming routine decisions into well-documented processes, business owners can navigate the complexities of daily operations with clarity and efficiency, ultimately preserving mental energy for strategic endeavors.

Other Time-Savers

AI has been a game changer for small business owners, completely transforming how we approach content creation. Its ability to automatically repurpose long-form content into bite-size pieces is a monumental time-saver. Take my podcast, for instance, which serves as my long-form content. By uploading the audio file into an AI tool, the platform works its magic, generating options for titles, show notes, social media content, emails, and more, all with minimal effort on my part. While I always go back to fine-tune the content, this process provides an excellent starting point for my content strategy. From chatbots to autoresponders seamlessly integrated into Instagram direct messages, AI applications open up avenues to reclaim hours in your day, empowering you to work smarter, not harder.

Email templates are a goldmine often overlooked in the realm of time-saving strategies. How often do you catch yourself responding to similar questions in your inbox? If you find yourself crafting a similar email more than once, I strongly recommend embracing the power of templates. Create a template with your standard reply, and customize it as needed. These templates can be updated whenever necessary, but the simple act of having them in place can save you substantial time in the daily email hustle. It's a small but impactful move toward efficiency in your communication workflows.

Action Item: Standard Operating Procedures

Map out your SOPs and identify opportunities for automation. After you have identified opportunities, begin to research potential automations to lighten your workload.

Chapter 6

You Can't Grow What You Don't Measure

Are your business decisions fueled by data or emotions? Tracking your key performance indicators (KPIs) is a strategic approach to uncovering what's effective and what's not within your business. By tracking data trends over time, you gain valuable insights into cash flow patterns, customer buying behaviors, and more. This wealth of information becomes the foundation for strategically planning your offers and launches.

Relying on data to guide your business decisions not only reduces stress but also helps diminish anxiety. It provides a bird's-eye view of your business's sales cycle, offering a comprehensive perspective rather than just a snapshot in time. KPIs play a fundamental role in assessing the return on investment for any financial commitments you've made. Additionally, they help track lead acquisition sources, allowing you to allocate your time and resources more efficiently into marketing channels that yield positive results.

One of my favorite examples of this comes from one of my business mentors, Jessica DeRose. Remember science class? You formed a hypothesis before you did an experiment. Running a business is essentially an experiment to figure out what works and what doesn't. No matter what results you get, good or bad, these results are not a reflection of you; they're simply data. As a business owner striving for desired results, the key is to embrace curiosity and dive into the data. Every challenge becomes surmountable when you analyze your numbers through an objective lens and identify the gaps in your business strategy.

Tracking the Data

The beauty of tracking KPIs lies in its flexibility—you can make it as straightforward or as intricate as you prefer; however, the more information you obtain, the more data you will have for strategic decision-making. If you're just starting out and this process feels overwhelming, begin with a few fundamental metrics and gradually expand based on your comfort level and business needs.

Fortunately, tracking your KPIs doesn't have to be a complex or time-consuming process. I find Google Sheets to be an excellent tool for this purpose. It offers accessibility for my team to input data monthly, and it can be set up to automate calculations, streamlining the process further.

The metrics you track can vary widely depending on your business, industry, and the platforms you use. To kick-start your tracking journey, here's a basic framework that you can adjust to meet your unique needs.

Cash Flow

- Income
  - Gross Revenue: This is the total amount of money coming into your account prior to any expenses.

Gross revenue provides a comprehensive snapshot of the total income before any expenses. Monitoring this KPI gives you a holistic view of your business's financial health.

- Further break this down by revenue source or product including:
  - affiliate income
  - monthly recurring revenue
  - new client sales versus return client sales
  - leading revenue source
  - low revenue source

This information helps you understand which streams contribute most significantly to your overall revenue so that you can strategically allocate resources, time, and effort. It helps you focus on the areas that bring in the most income, optimize your business strategy for maximum profitability, and identify potential areas of improvement that can mitigate risks and prevent revenue loss.

- Expenses
  - What are your recurring monthly and yearly expenses?
  - What are your other business expenses, including taxes, insurance, supplies, etc.?

o   Of these expenses, which are essential?

o   What could you eliminate that you no longer use?

Tracking this data helps differentiate between essential and non-essential expenses and allows you to prioritize spending on critical aspects of your business while identifying opportunities to streamline your budget and keep more money in your pocket.

- Break-Even Point: This is the point at which your revenue covers all of your expenses. Monitoring this metric ensures that your business remains financially viable.

  o   In order to calculate your break-even point, add up all your expenses, including both recurring monthly and yearly costs. Once you have this total, divide it by 12 to determine the exact amount of revenue needed to cover your business expenses on a monthly basis. While this figure may vary monthly due to the timing of yearly expenses, it serves as a reliable indicator of whether you're on track to achieve profitability. Consulting with a CPA to establish a budget tailored to your specific situation is a wise step in ensuring financial stability and success.

- Net Revenue

  o   Gross sales minus expenses

Net revenue represents the actual income after deducting all expenses, offering a clear picture of profitability.

- Gross Profit Margin
    - Gross profit divided by net revenue x 100

Tracking your gross profit margin allows you to identify how efficiently your business is converting sales into profit, which aids in streamlining operation and maximizing the return on sales.

- Monthly Profit/Loss
    - Did you hit your target?

This metric helps in identifying areas of success and potential improvement, facilitating strategic decision-making.

Note: If you do not have a CPA yet, this is one area I strongly encourage you to outsource. Tax laws are constantly changing and without a trusted adviser, you can easily make a mistake, costing you time and money.

Lead Generation

- New Inquiries/Leads
    - How many potential clients inquired about your products or services?

A consistent flow of inquiries indicates an interest in your products or services.

- Referral Source
    - How are these clients discovering you?

The easiest way to figure this out? Ask! This allows you to strategically adjust your marketing efforts and calculate the ROI on any paid marketing campaigns so that you can evaluate which marketing channels and strategies are resonating with your target audience.

- Discovery Calls
  - o How many leads booked a discovery call to discuss your services?

High levels of new inquiries suggest strong customer engagement.

- Conversion Rate
  - o How many of the discovery call conversations led to sales?

It is critical to leverage this information when mapping out your sales plan. For example, if I need to secure a minimum of three new clients to break even in a given month, I know that, on average, I will need to be on a minimum of six calls to achieve this goal. Armed with knowledge about discovery call conversion rates, you can make informed strategic decisions. Whether adjusting pricing, refining messaging, or targeting specific market segments, this data guides decisions that impact your business's growth.

- Qualified Leads
  - o Are those reaching out to you qualified leads, especially those that do not convert to a client?

Leads are great. However, if they're not leading to sales, you're fighting an uphill battle. An abnormal number of rejections and unqualified leads can indicate a potential messaging issue in your content. This data prompts a closer examination of how you communicate your offers, ensuring that your message resonates effectively with the right audience.

- If the lead does not convert to a customer, what objections do they have?

Use this data to get ahead of objections in your content and messaging. Having awareness of potential objections is a strategic advantage in sales as it empowers you to navigate conversations more effectively, build trust, and tailor your approach to meet the specific needs and concerns of your audience, ultimately leading to increased sales success.

- New Clients Obtained

Similar to conversion rate, tracking this metric over time allows you to see the natural ebb and flow of your customers' buying patterns.

- Current Client Total or Waitlist Size

Business owners can tailor their marketing strategies based on the current client total. If there is room for growth, marketing efforts can focus on attracting new clients.

- Capacity for Growth
  - Based on your current client total, what is your capacity to add more clients?

Knowing your overall capacity is extremely important to managing your time effectively. There will be a limit to how much you can achieve on your own without outsourcing. In order to increase your income when you reach capacity, you will need to do one of three things: increase your pricing, decrease your overhead, or adjust your offers.

- Average Sales Cycle Length
  - How long does it take for someone to move from a follower to a buyer?

Understanding the sales cycle duration from follower to buyer empowers business owners to strategically plan content and gain a more accurate sales prediction.

- Current Client Retention Rate
  - How many clients am I retaining from month to month?

This information allows you to see how much time and energy you need to devote to lead generation and can help you strategically plan out your offers and launches. A high customer retention rate contributes to revenue stability because repeat customers consistently contribute to sales, providing a steady and predictable income stream.

Email List

- Total List Size

This metric provides a baseline for assessing the overall reach of your email campaigns and can help guide decisions on list expansion strategies and audience targeting.

- Total Emails Sent

Assists in resource planning in order to leverage your email platform.

- New Subscribers

Shows the overall growth of your list.

- Opt-Ins per Lead Magnet

Measures the effectiveness of lead magnets in attracting new subscribers and helps guide future content creation.

- Unsubscribes
  - What email triggered the unsubscribe?

Identifies potential issues with content or frequency.

- Open Rate
  - What percentage of subscribers are opening the emails you send?
  - Which emails have the highest open rate?

This monitors the effectiveness of subject lines and highlights which resonate with your subscribers. Industry standards vary depending on the source, but 30 percent is considered average.

- Click-Through Rate
  - What percentage of subscribers are clicking on links in the emails you send?
  - What links are subscribers clicking on?

This identifies popular content to assist in planning future campaigns in order to leverage your email platform. A click-through rate of 10 percent is exceptional.

- Percentage Growth

Measures the overall growth trajectory of your email list.

Website

- Website Traffic: Total Views

Provides an overview of overall website visibility and effectiveness of marketing efforts in driving traffic to the website.

- New Traffic

Identifies new visitors to the website.

- Traffic Source

Pinpoints the origin of website traffic, necessary information for refining marketing strategies.

- Bounce Rate

Indicates the percentage of visitors who leave without interacting further. High bounce rates may signal issues with website content, user experience, or relevance to visitor expectations.

- Highest Visited Page

Identifies the most popular and engaging content on your website by highlighting topics or pages that resonate with your audience.

Podcast and YouTube

- Downloads Total (All Time)

Indicates the overall popularity and growth of your podcast and helps evaluate the success of individual episodes and overall content strategy.

- Downloads Monthly
  - Percentage Growth

Provides insights into the effectiveness of promotional efforts and audience engagement, and monitors month-to-month growth in downloads.

Note: Podcast downloads via YouTube are not often calculated into overall downloads on most podcast hosting platforms

- Unique Listeners

Identifies the number of distinct individuals listening to your podcast to allow for a more accurate assessment of your podcast's reach and impact.

- New Subscribers
  - o Percentage Growth

Indicates the growth of your subscriber base and helps tailor content to retain and attract new listeners.

- Top Three Downloaded Episodes
  - o 30 Day
  - o 60 Day
  - o 90 Day

Leveraging this data is helpful in creating content that your listeners want to hear and will be more likely to share because it highlights episodes with the highest listener engagement.

- New Reviews

Reflects audience feedback and sentiment and provides insights for improvement.

- Listen Notes Global Rank

Indicates your podcast's standing in a global context.

Social Media

Social media strategies are constantly changing, and new platforms are always being created; therefore, the specific metrics you track will vary by platform. Utilize the robust analytics available on most platforms by using a business account in order to obtain the data.

- Follower Total

Provides an overview of your social media audience size, demonstrating the potential impact of your social media efforts.

- New Followers

Indicates the success of your strategies in attracting new followers and helps guide decisions on content, campaigns, and engagement tactics.

- Engagement Rate

Organic reach varies by platform; therefore, this metric is even more important than your follower counts when assessing the effectiveness of your social media content. The more your content is engaged with, saved, and shared, the more the algorithm pushes your content out to your audience.

- Growth Percentage as Compared to the Previous Month

Shows the month-to-month growth of your social media following and provides insights into the impact of your strategies and the overall impact of your social media presence.

- High Performing Content
  - o Most Shared
  - o Most Saved

When you know what content is performing well, leverage this information to repurpose the high performing content. You can change the graphic, colors, or font, or simply re-post the same content. As much as we like to think everyone is paying attention, most are just scrolling by. Use the data and work smarter, not harder.

Focus on Less, Achieve More

If you're not getting the results you desire, analyzing your KPIs eliminates the guesswork, allowing you to identify what you could do differently and then to adjust your focus. When you develop a concentrated strategy, you actually end up achieving more because you have focused your energy. Think of your business as a puzzle, with each piece representing a different aspect of your strategy. When the overall picture isn't coming together as expected, analyzing your KPIs is like examining each puzzle piece. It's about understanding the shape, color, and cut of each piece to ensure they easily fit into place.

Now, imagine trying to solve multiple puzzles at once, scattering pieces from each one on the table—a confusing jumble leading to incomplete pictures. However, if you focus on assembling one puzzle at a time, taking the time to connect each piece deliberately, you not only complete each puzzle successfully but also in a more efficient manner.

Tracking the Wins

Have you ever found yourself stuck in the web of "When-Then" thinking? It's a trap many of us fall into, a pattern of conditional living where we postpone actions and goals until certain conditions are met. "When I have more money, then I'll start paying myself." "When I find the time, then I'll start tracking my numbers." The list is endless, and the consequences of such thinking can be profound.

The trap of this mindset lies in the perpetual cycle of setting goals, achieving them, and promptly moving the goalpost to the next unattained aspiration. The dissatisfaction persists, and the cycle repeats. The danger is in reaching the end of your journey and realizing you spent a lifetime chasing an ever-elusive sense of fulfillment.

With a never-ending to-do list, it's easy to lose sight of the progress you have made along the way. I encourage you to pause not just when you reach the finish line, but to celebrate the small wins. Tracking and celebrating your accomplishments provides tangible proof of progress to your brain, especially during those moments when it seems like nothing is falling into place. It triggers a surge of dopamine, a feel-good chemical that becomes your ally, motivating you to persevere.

Remember, every step moves you forward. While you might not be exactly where you envisioned by now, release the grip of expectations and embrace the current moment. The joy is in the journey. Celebrate your courage in facing challenges head-on and making decisions that once seemed daunting.

Every twist and turn has led you to this very point, equipped with the skills to create the life you've envisioned.

Celebrate not just the destination, but the path you're traveling—the progress, the lessons, and the resilience that shape your story. Let each win be a beacon of light during moments of doubt, proof that you can succeed time and again, fueled by your commitment and hard work.

You have survived every challenge and obstacle along the way. Maybe things didn't go as you had hoped, but you are here, stronger, more resilient, and equipped with knowledge because you handled it. Don't give up on the person you are becoming. When nothing is certain, everything is possible. And that's a fact of life: the only thing certain in life is uncertainty. There are no guarantees that one day you will retire, that one day you will have enough time, that one day you will have enough money . . . This pattern of thinking keeps us living in the future when the only thing for certain is this moment right now.

Action Item: Track Your KPIs

Start tracking your KPIs, successes, and accomplishments. Start a list of wins. Screenshot amazing testimonials and save them in a folder on your computer or phone. Track your features, and make note of the networking events you attended. Celebrate every single win along the way. Focus on what you did accomplish versus what you didn't complete.

Download a free KPI tracker at **amytraugh.com/ceobook**

Chapter 7

Just Because You Can . . .

We spend our days engulfed in busyness. We're so busy being busy that we forget this fundamental truth: how we spend our time is a choice. The next time you hear yourself saying, "I don't have the time," I challenge you to rephrase it as, "This doesn't matter to me right now." The power to choose lies in your hands, and it's your responsibility to choose wisely. If something genuinely matters, you'll find the time; if not, you'll find excuses. Picture being offered a million dollars for completing a specific task—chances are, you'd make it happen.

We often spend our energy on trivial tasks, seeking a false sense of control. For instance, have you ever found yourself cleaning out your closet instead of writing that pivotal email or tackling another task that propels you toward your goals? Fun fact: I was absolutely guilty of this one when writing this book.

Ultimately, just because we can do something doesn't mean we should. Are we genuinely valuing our most precious assets—time and energy? Sometimes, energy leaks occur because we're not investing our time judiciously, and this oversight can cost us money. It's about scrutinizing how we spend our time and prioritizing tasks that push us toward our goals, rather than making excuses and attributing our current reality to external factors. At the day's end, the results we achieve are a direct reflection of our actions.

The Juggle of Time and Money

The thought of asking for help and outsourcing can feel completely terrifying, especially if you identify with being a bit of a type A control enthusiast like myself. I encourage you to take a deep breath. I get it. I swear, it gets easier. If I can do it, so can you. Here's the silver lining—the more you dip your toes into outsourcing, the easier the process becomes. Reframing my perspective on the juggle between time, money, and business growth has brought about tangible changes. Yes, there might be a price tag attached, but what I gain in return—time and energy—makes it all worthwhile. It allows me to zero in on the high-impact tasks that truly propel my business forward.

With each step in this direction, not only do you regain time, but you also open the door to possibilities that can take your business to the next level. Consider it an investment in the future of your business. It's in acknowledging the value of your time that you can make choices that set the stage for sustained success.

Outsourcing: Where to Start?

Outsourcing tasks around your home is an easy place to start and often doesn't involve an exchange of money. Take a few minutes to set up automatic bill pay so you don't have to take the time each month to schedule recurring payments. Ask your family to help you with day-to-day tasks like cooking, laundry, and dishes. Trying to do it all makes us feel seen and important and because of this we end up wearing busy like a badge of honor. Spoiler alert: you don't get bonus points because you didn't want to ask for help.

Short on time? Try grocery delivery or pickup. This alone saves me an hour and a half each time I use it. Think about it: 15 minutes to the store, an hour in the store, and 15 minutes driving home. By having my groceries delivered, I have saved myself an hour and a half that I could spend on IPAs. Yes, there may be a small fee attached to using this service, but I have found I actually save money because I only get what is on the list, which is saved, by the way, for future orders. I'm not tempted to throw in the random delicious box of Pop-Tarts or Oreos longingly staring at me on the end cap. Those delectable delights would get me every time. We all have our kryptonite, right?

Cleaning is another area that can be outsourced in order to save time and energy. My new mantra: if you don't enjoy it, outsource it! I am literally giving myself back hours because I can spend my time on areas that will generate income versus scrubbing floors and dusting.

These are just a few of the countless ways to buy back your time. Consider mobile oil changes, lawn care services, laundry services . . . there are so many possibilities. Time is finite, energy is finite, but money is infinite. There will always be ways to make more money; however, there are only 24 hours in a given day.

Speed Up Your Results

Once you have gotten used to the art of delegation, let's look at outsourcing tasks within your business. The objective is clear: outsource anything that falls below your hourly rate. By doing so, you free up valuable time to focus on high-impact activities that truly move the needle in your business, ensuring that every minute spent contributes significantly to your goals.

Grab a piece of paper and write down everything you do throughout the day to run your business. I suggest using the information from your time audit in Part One to help. Next to each item, I want you to indicate how you feel about each task. Do you like performing the task, dislike performing the task, or feel neutral about the task?

Start with the items you dislike. Which of these tasks are things that do not need to be done by you? Get these off your list ASAP! It will feel like you're literally taking a load off of your shoulders. Freeing up the invisible mental load that's holding you down creates more time to focus on doing the things you love. I encourage you to delegate items that don't need to be done by you and those tasks that you're doing because you feel like you "should be" doing them. You can't be doing your best work if you're doing *all* the work.

Your job is to establish priorities in your life and in your business. Anything you want in this world can be achieved if you make it a priority, but everything can't be a priority. Outsourcing speeds your results.

Boundaries: Stop Letting Your Business Run You

You didn't quit your 9-to-5 to work 24-7. Establishing boundaries is necessary to creating a sustainable business so you don't find yourself on the fast track to burnout. You're setting expectations to others of how you expect to be treated. Boundaries protect your time because, without boundaries, you are allowing others to dictate how you're spending your time. Answering emails and messages at every hour of the day shows others that you are essentially "on call." When you create and maintain boundaries, you start living a life on your terms and begin to release the endless cycle of people-pleasing.

If we don't take the time to recharge ourselves, we will deplete our energy and then we can't help anyone. A great example that illustrates the importance of taking the time to recharge is your cell phone. What happens when the power level drops below 20 percent? The indicator turns red, telling you that you need to charge your phone soon. If you don't charge it before it gets to zero, what happens? The phone shuts off and won't work.

Boundaries help you hold yourself accountable and keep the promises you made to yourself by respecting your time. They decrease the excuses that stop you from taking the action needed to create the life you desire. They also protect your inner peace. Boundaries aren't just a way to keep things that don't matter out, they're a way to say yes to yourself and stay in alignment with your values. This gives us the freedom to focus on the things that matter to us, not what others deem important for us.

Another way that can help you to maintain your boundaries, especially if you are working from home, is by creating a physical space for your work tasks. With advances in technology, many of us have the ability to work anytime and anywhere. This has blurred the lines between work and life. All too often, we end up spending hours on end staring at a screen and missing the beautiful life playing out in front of us.

When you create a designated workspace, whether a corner of your home or an entire office, this area is devoted solely to work. This also serves as a reminder to others that when you are in your work area, your focus is on work. You may need to put your phone on airplane mode or throw on headphones—do whatever you need to do. When you are working from home, it's really easy to get sidetracked and put the things that would move the needle forward in your business on the back burner. Boundaries keep you on track.

Establishing Boundaries

Start by looking at your schedule and mark down your start and stop times. These are the "bookends" of my day, and once I am done working, I am done. This has allowed me to regain control of my life and actually get things done because now I have limited the amount of time to complete the task.

This may be a block of six hours or this may be two one-hour blocks; whatever time you are able to dedicate solely to focusing on your business gets blocked off. Using these blocks of time, schedule your nonnegotiable items first. The really beautiful part of running a business is that you get to have the flexibility to build a business around your life. I encourage you to schedule tasks around the periods of time when you have the most energy.

Don't be surprised if you discover that you have more on your plate than there are hours in the day. Awareness is the first step to reframing your expectations and subsequently asking for help so that you can achieve the results you desire. You get to decide how to use your time.

Time Expansion

When I first started my business, my youngest was in preschool and I had exactly two and a half hours to get everything accomplished. Looking back, I rocked it! I can't believe how much I would accomplish in such a short period of time. I figured that when both of the kids were in school for six hours a day, I would get even more done. I would make so much progress because I would have three times as many hours to get through my to-do list. It turned out that I was completely wrong. The six hours devoted to building my business would fly by and I'd find myself getting very little accomplished.

Turns out there is a whole theory behind this. It's called Parkinson's Law. Parkinson's Law is the concept that the task at hand will expand to fill the time given to complete it. This is exactly why I wasn't making as much progress as I thought I would when I moved from two and a half hours of time to six hours of time.

Learning to Say No

Boundaries are easy to establish, yet hard to maintain. Want to know the easiest way to maintain them? Learn to say no to anything that falls outside of the boundaries you have set. If you're a recovering people pleaser, like me, this is easier said than done. Just as with any new skill, it takes practice to master.

Here are a few of my favorite ways to say no.

- "I appreciate the offer, but I'm unable to commit to that right now."
- "Thank you for thinking of me, but I won't be able to participate."
- "I need to decline, but I'm grateful for the invitation."
- "I'm afraid I have other commitments at the moment."

- "I've got a lot on my plate at the moment, so I have to pass this time."
- "I'm currently not taking on any new responsibilities, but I appreciate you reaching out."
- "I'm honored you asked, but unfortunately, I won't be able to."
- "I have to respectfully decline this opportunity. Thank you for understanding."

"No" is a complete sentence. You do not owe anyone an explanation and do not need to justify yourself. I get it; the feeling of guilt is real. However, it is just that—a feeling. Guilt is a self-inflicted feeling deeply rooted in our beliefs, created because you believe that saying or doing something will upset someone else or let them down. It makes us feel incredibly uncomfortable and, therefore, we would rather hold ourselves back than disappoint others.

Action Item: The Art of Delegation

List all the tasks you perform throughout the day, labeling them as "love," "hate," or "neutral." Starting with the list of items that you hate, highlight those items that don't require you to perform the task. Begin to delegate those items.

Chapter 8

Are You Treating Your Business Like a Business?

A business plan is one of the most foundational, yet overlooked, elements that will help you when building a business. A business plan acts as a living, breathing guide to provide structure and keep you in alignment and on track to reach your goals. Remember, structure creates freedom.

In order to build a business that you can scale, you need a solid foundation because you can't build a skyscraper on quicksand. If you desire to have your business serve as your primary source of income, you can't dip your toe in and show up when you feel like it.

Here is an overview of what you can include in your business plan.

- Business Overview

Outline your mission, vision, and values using the information you obtained in Chapter 3.

- Management Plan

Outline your role and each employee's role within the company, including subcontractors. Clearly communicating each team member's roles and responsibilities allows you to create a well-oiled business machine.

- Operations Plan

Include all SOPs and workflows that you outlined in Chapter 5. An outline of your daily nonnegotiables and lists of weekly, monthly, quarterly, and semiannual tasks keep you organized so nothing slips through the cracks. In addition, I find it helpful to include my tech stack here, listing all of the platforms I use to complete various tasks within the business.

- Financial Plan

Use the information from Chapter 6 to map out your financial plan. Include your budget, operating expenses, sales goals, and product suite. In addition, I include my big dreams and investments list. This is an ongoing list of investments I plan to make, including conferences, platforms, courses, etc.

- Reverse Engineering Your Goals

When you know where you're at and know where you desire to be, you can reverse engineer the sales needed to achieve your goal by determining exactly how much of your product or service you will need to sell to meet the goal you have set.

Breaking this goal down by month and week allows your goals to feel achievable.

In addition, make sure that you have a product suite that supports your sales goals. For example, if your goal is to make $10K a month and your only offer is a $10-per-month membership, you will need to have 1,000 people in your membership in order to meet your sales goal. If your goal is the same $10K a month and you offer a group program at $2,000, you would only need to sell five seats in your program to achieve your goals.

- Sales and Marketing Plan

Using the information you obtained regarding your ideal client in Chapter 3, you can easily create a sales and marketing plan to help you achieve your goals. We will break this down step by step in Part Three, but here's an overview of what your customer journey will look like.

Visibility: create awareness and attract ideal clients.

Authority: build "know, like, and trust" with ideal clients through clear messaging in order to move to a list you own.

Nurture: build relationships with ideal clients who have opted in.

Sell: demonstrate the value of your product or service and present the custom solution to a problem.

Customer Experience: let your customers be your best salespeople by focusing on retention and referrals.

CEO Quarterly Review

Now that you have created a business plan, don't let it get lost in a random folder on your computer, never to be seen again. Your business plan should be a living, breathing document that keeps you on track.

As the CEO of your business, you need to make the time to regularly review your numbers. One way to ensure you stay on track to achieve your goals is through a CEO quarterly review. This process gives you the opportunity to assess the progress you have made over the past three months, assess your current situation, and develop a plan to help you make adjustments so that you can reach your goals in the most time efficient manner. The information you gathered in Chapter 3 will make performing your CEO quarterly review much easier.

Self-Assessment:

How am I feeling?

How's my energy level?

Am I maintaining my boundaries?

Am I asking for help when needed?

Am I noticing any signs of burnout?

Do my "yeses" feel aligned with my mission, vision, and values?

Am I holding myself accountable and completing my daily nonnegotiable items?

Review of Numbers and Metrics (Looking Back)

What worked well?

Profit/Loss report:

- What is my current overhead?
- What was my gross income?
- What was my profit margin?
- What was the ROI on any investments?
- What was my top-grossing product or service?

Metrics review (KPIs): refer back to Chapter 6

- Email List
- Social Media
- Podcast
- Website

Systems and workflows

- Are all SOPs and workflows up to date?
- Can I identify any opportunities for additional automation?

- Does anything need to be outsourced?
- How has communication with my team been?
- Are clear roles and responsibilities established?
- Are there any recurring issues that need to be addressed?
- What is my current capacity for expansion?

Acquisition and Conversion

Consultation calls:

Total new inquiries:

Conversion rate:

Leading objection:

Number of new clients:

Current openings or wait list:

How did I get in front of my ideal clients?

What was my leading client acquisition source?

Am I attracting aligned clients?

What did I launch?

What were my daily nonnegotiables and IPAs?

Strategic Planning (Looking Ahead)

What is my primary focus going to be?

What are my top three daily nonnegotiables for the next quarter?

Do I need to outsource anything?

What will I be launching or what product or service will I focus on?

What will my launch runway be?

Do I need a new lead magnet/opt-in?

What is my gross revenue target for the upcoming quarter?

Do my offers and current pricing support my revenue goals?

What opportunities exist for improvement?

How can I better handle objections?

What investments do I want to make?

Things I want to learn:

People I want to collaborate with:

Upcoming events I want to attend:

Crazy big ideas (dream BIG!):

This may seem like a daunting task at first; however, the process becomes faster and easier each time you go through it. Schedule a time on your calendar and hold yourself accountable, because at the end of the day, you are the CEO of your business. Leverage the data and you will save time and energy.

Action Item: Make a Plan

Download your free Business Plan Template, CEO Quarterly Review, and Business Foundation Checklist by visiting **amytraugh.com/ceobook**

Part Three: Organic Marketing and Sales, From Follower to Buyer

Sales isn't merely about transactions; it's about strategically positioning yourself in front of individuals who genuinely need the solution you provide and understand that you are the perfect answer to their unique challenges. Mapping a detailed customer journey serves as a strategic guide to transforming casual followers into enthusiastic buyers. We'll walk through each of these components in the upcoming chapters.

Chapter 9

Get Seen!

Goal: Create awareness to attract aligned clients.

Lead Generation Simplified

An incredible product or service is just one piece of your business; the real challenge is ensuring that the right people know you exist. If no one knows that you exist, how will you make sales? Your mission is to capture the attention of your ideal clients because visibility is what generates leads. Playing small doesn't serve anyone, and there's someone out there right now in need of the solution you offer. The first step to making sales is creating awareness that resonates with aligned clients.

Visibility Opportunities

It's time to make the most of the valuable insights you've gathered about your ideal clients in Chapter 3. By taking the time to truly understand your ideal client—their challenges, their desires, and the barriers they face—you've armed yourself with a strategic advantage for lead generation. This clarity acts as a guiding light, directing your lead generation efforts with purpose and effectiveness to connect authentically with your audience.

Your ideal clients are out there, and your job is to identify where they spend their time, strategically aligning with your target demographic in the places that matter. For example, if your ideal clients are senior citizens, Instagram might not be the optimal platform to connect with them. Although exceptions exist, the key is to strategically focus on meeting your clients in the places where they naturally gravitate versus trying to be everywhere. In a world full of noise, you must amplify your message to cut through the clutter. This is not the time to follow trends or mimic everyone else.

The following list will provide you with extensive visibility opportunities that you can use to begin the lead generation process.

- Your Website

A website is a useful business tool to provide information on the services and products that you provide. Make sure to modify your website for search engine optimization (SEO) to improve its chances of appearing in search results using relevant keywords. I wish it were that easy, but there is an entire strategy dedicated to improving SEO that goes into achieving a ranked status on Google Search.

Google Analytics is a free platform that, when connected to your website, will help you track website traffic, user behavior, common search terms, and other essential metrics to further leverage industry-specific keywords in your content that your ideal clients may be searching for online.

Utilize your website as a place to establish an online presence, provide information related to your products and services, and share free resources to build your email list.

Bonus tip: create a page on your website that resembles a Linktree unique to each social media platform to monitor the traffic you receive from social media.

- Google Maps Business Profile (formerly Google my Business)

If you are a local service provider or have a brick-and-mortar location, a Google Maps listing is a completely free and easy way to get seen in Google's top search results. When someone enters a search term (near me) the top three businesses that provide that search term for a specific location will appear.

By claiming and optimizing your Google Maps Business Profile, you provide accurate and up-to-date information about your business, such as address, phone number, business hours, and website. Ratings and reviews left by customers on your listing will improve your business reputation and help you rank higher in search results.

- Social Media

Social media is certainly a piece of the puzzle, but proceed with caution. This should not be your entire visibility strategy as organic reach—the amount of accounts that see your content without paid promotion—is only 3 to 5 percent on average, depending on the platform (at the time of publication).

The goal of social media should be to move potential customers or clients to a list you own, a.k.a. your email list, by providing value and building relationships. You do not own your social media accounts. The platform has the ability to shut your account down at any time for any reason, or your account could get hacked. This can, and unfortunately does, happen quite often. Always have your two-factor authentication enabled. I get it—it's a pain.

Consistency is key when it comes to social media. It gives business owners the opportunity to humanize their brand, build community, and build relationships with potential customers. By fostering engagement through polls, responding to comments, and encouraging discussions, businesses can create a loyal following that actively supports and shares their content, expanding reach organically.

- Reframing Our Relationship with Social Media

It's easy to get caught up in the cycle of comparison on social media, therefore it's important to reframe our relationship with it. View social media as a vehicle that can be used as an opportunity to collaborate and connect with others, to share value, and to act as an active contributor.

In the world of social media, you can portray any persona you want. Someone can create the illusion that all they do is sit on a beach on vacation and drive a car that costs more than a decent-size home. You don't know what is actually happening on the other side. How big is their ad spend? What's the overhead they have to run their business? How many silent launches have they had that they don't like to talk about? We're only seeing the side of others that they want us to see, and that sucks us into the world of deceptive marketing strategies and unethical sales tactics which have created a bad name for an entire industry.

Remember, there is not a limited number of seats at the table of success. Seeing someone else achieve their goals doesn't take away from your opportunity to shine and succeed as well. Don't give up on your dreams because you see someone else doing what you desire. Your message could be the missing piece to move someone forward. Comparison is merely a survival mechanism our brain uses to keep us safe.

- A Note on Pinterest and YouTube

While these two platforms can technically be considered social media, they are essentially massive search engines. Type a search term into Google and chances are that YouTube and Pinterest results will appear somewhere in your search results. This allows businesses to tap into their vast user base that's actively searching for information, tutorials, reviews, and more.

These platforms house evergreen content that remains relevant over time and can continue to attract views, subscribers, and engagement, providing ongoing exposure for the business long after posting, versus platforms like Facebook and Instagram where the average life cycle of content is 24 to 48 hours.

With the influx of new platforms being created, I caution you to not spread yourself too thin. Remember to focus on the platforms where your ideal clients are spending the most time. When you're trying to be everywhere, you end up overwhelmed and don't show up anywhere.

- Podcast Guesting

Podcast guesting is a fabulous way to expand your reach when leveraged appropriately. Podcasts often have niche audiences interested in specific topics or industries. Being a guest on a podcast with a mutually aligned audience allows you to directly reach new potential clients, thereby expanding your visibility and creating cross-promotional opportunities. This is a perfect place to share your opt-ins to grow your email list. It also enhances credibility because you are showing up as an authority in your field by sharing your expertise and insights. One of the biggest perks? Podcast episodes remain accessible over time, providing a lasting impact on visibility. Even older episodes can continue to attract new listeners, contributing to sustained visibility.

- Media Features

Yes, getting featured on the cover of *Time* magazine would be really cool, but unless you're Mark Cuban-level, the chances are slim that you will be gracing it anytime soon.

Wouldn't it be cool, though? Media features are a powerful way to grow brand awareness, reach a wider audience, and build authority. If you are a local service provider, seek out media opportunities for publications that your target client is consuming. The easiest way to get featured? Just ask! When pitching yourself to media outlets, it's important that you are clear and concise in your pitch and communicate the value that you will provide to the outlet in exchange for the feature.

- Client Referral Programs

We'll get into the power of referral and word of mouth later in Part Three. The best way to get more referrals? Ask! Client referrals are a targeted approach that further enhances the effectiveness of your visibility efforts with minimal effort on your end.

- Speaking Engagements

These are great opportunities because they position you as an expert in your field in front of a targeted audience. Sharing insights, knowledge, and experiences during a presentation establishes the speaker as an expert, attracting attention and interest and providing a direct avenue for interacting with a live audience. As a speaker, you are often featured in event promotions, agendas, and marketing materials, further enhancing your visibility. Social media posts generate excitement, and attendees may share, comment, or engage with the content, broadening its reach. Speaking engagements create opportunities to collect leads through sign-ups, inquiries, or post-presentation discussions and often lead to word-of-mouth referrals, which can contribute to organic growth.

- Giveaways

Who doesn't love winning a contest? Giveaways and contests, especially those done in collaboration with others, can be great visibility opportunities to create brand awareness. Consider requiring contestants to provide their email address or share with a friend in order to enter as a way to further boost your visibility. By engaging with the contest, participants become more invested in your business and its offerings.

- Virtual Master Classes and Webinars

There's a reason big industry leaders typically have a free master class leading up to a launch. It's to provide massive value and position themselves as a thought leader and as an authority in their field. By giving others a taste of what you do, you'll grow your list and your audience. Hosting free sessions provides an opportunity to receive feedback and improve future offers. Inviting additional guest speakers or collaborating with influencers for the master class can further expand the audience. In addition, recordings of the master class can be repurposed for ongoing content creation.

Community and Collaboration

Community and collaboration have gained significant attention in the online space in recent years. Recognizing the challenges of building a business, we've come to understand that collaboration is more impactful than competition. It enables us to link arms, pool our resources, tap into each other's strengths, and create more substantial influence. Consider the industry leaders; those at the top are often collaborating, endorsing each other's endeavors and events. They realize they won't resonate with everyone, whereas those at the bottom are often operating from a scarcity mindset and constantly spending their precious time and energy competing with one another.

No matter how saturated the market feels, infinite possibilities exist, leaving room for your unique voice, talent, life experiences, and perspectives. The scarcity often perceived is rooted in false narratives we tell ourselves, shaped by our beliefs. Fellow professionals in your field are not competitors but resources, challenging you to think differently and show up authentically.

The collective strength of individuals shining together brightens our shared path, providing mutual support through challenges. By standing together, we become a beacon for those who have dimmed their light due to societal pressures. True happiness lies in helping others reach their highest potential.

Success in your business journey requires three types of people in your world. You need those ahead of you acting as trailblazers, offering proof of what's possible. They will stretch you and challenge you to dream bigger and do bigger. Get into their world, borrow the belief from them, and learn from them because they started at ground zero just like you.

You need those alongside you who understand where you are in the journey of entrepreneurship. Link arms with those who are walking beside you—they understand the challenges, they will call you out when you're slacking, they will keep you going when you're tempted to quit, and they will pick you up when you fall down. Many people in your life, including your loved ones, won't understand what you are doing and may even question you. At first, this used to trigger me. Now I realize that this was coming from a place of love. They were trying to keep me safe and wanted me to maintain my old identity as I evolved. As you move forward, there will be parts of you that you need to shed in order to step into your purpose and potential.

Finally, there are those behind you. Help them. Make their journey a little lighter. The entrepreneurial journey can feel lonely, but your people are out there, and it is your job to find them.

A perfect illustration of the power of community and collaboration is a story included in the book *The Secrets of Successful Selling Habits* by Zig Ziglar.[5]

A man came home one evening, and his seven-year-old son was doing a little work out in the backyard. He was building a fort. There was one heavy post the youngster was trying to move, struggling and straining and trying so hard to lift it.

His dad watched him for a couple of minutes and said, "Son, use all your strength." The little boy looked up and said,

---

5. Zig Ziglar, *The Secrets of Successful Selling Habits* (New York, NY: G&D Media, 2019).

"Daddy, you know I'm trying. I am using all of my strength."
The dad said, "No, son, you're not using all your strength."
"Yes, I am! I tried hard." "Well, son, you didn't ask me to help
you. You didn't use my strength."

No matter how brilliant your mind or strategy is, if you're
playing a solo game, you'll always lose out to a team.

A Crazy Collaboration Idea . . . That Worked!

At the beginning of 2023, I knew that I needed to grow my
visibility in order to grow my business. I had a crazy idea and
it actually worked. I knew that in order to get seen, I needed
to collaborate with others. But how was I going to do this?
What value did I have to share that would help others? I had
a podcast, and people love to be a guest on a podcast. Those
guests have followers and, most of the time, love to share
that they were on a podcast . . . and that was the moment the
lightbulb went off.

I set a goal to create five episodes a week for at least a month.
I put a call for guests out into the world and boy, did the
world respond. I had my month booked, and I met the most
incredible women. I was having so much fun that I decided
to continue this until the end of Q1 which turned into Q2 and
then Q3. I eventually scaled back to three times a week at
the start of Q4. What did this accomplish? Massive visibility,
podcast swaps, and collaboration opportunities. Because I
was able to offer value and grow my network, my audience
grew and, therefore, my sales grew, all because of the power
of networking. (Disclaimer: I have a team on the backend

that edits and uploads my podcast. Please do not attempt this strategy without support.)

Standing Out in a Noisy World

What if I told you there's a straightforward way to consistently attract your ideal client across any platform? It boils down to one simple thing: being authentically yourself. Yes, it's that easy. By embracing your true self, you naturally draw in your ideal clients. In a world filled with noise, standing out requires you to be outstanding. Ditch the trends and filters in the online space; being trendy makes you blend in, but removing the filter and standing up for who you are makes you stand out from the crowd. Your mission is to make an impact, and blending in makes you part of the noise.

Consider this: what captures your attention? It's things that are unique, that stand out, and provoke thought. In a world saturated with trends, your ability to show up as yourself becomes attention-grabbing. You want to be outstanding and therefore stand out from the crowd.

Stand out by taking a stand and being different. Your objective is to attract ideal clients and repel those who don't align with your values because you're not meant to be for everyone. Even Taylor Swift has her share of critics. Trends, more often than not, lead to uniformity, making you indistinguishable from the crowd. Be a trendsetter, not a trend follower, to set yourself apart.

Leaning into authenticity not only attracts your ideal clients but also builds trust. It lifts the invisible burden created by trying to be someone you're not, aligning you with your vision and values. You transform into an innovator and thought leader, breaking away from the crowd fearlessly. It's time to take a stand and be you because what you bring to the table matters.

No matter how many times an idea has been shared, we haven't heard your take on it. Your unique perspective makes a difference. There's always room for you. We often count ourselves out, seeing others living the life we desire. Instead, see it as proof that it's possible. Whatever you want—whatever it looks like for you—is within reach.

Consider this book. In a bookstore filled with personal development and business strategy titles, there isn't one authored by Amy Traugh—until now. I'm sharing my story and the strategies I personally use with clients to help them achieve the success they desire. While many ideas in this book aren't groundbreaking, they haven't been shared from my perspective. My goal is that in reading this book, a fellow entrepreneur will have the strategy and mindset they need to live a life they desire.

It's easy to say "just be yourself," but it's far more challenging to do it, due to the fear of judgment, which we'll explore further in Part Four. The reality is, you won't be for everyone. You will be misunderstood, not everyone will agree with you, and not everyone will like you. Your job is not to be for everyone. This is YOUR journey.

The key to lead generation is to get loud, stay consistent, and leverage the power of community and collaboration to get seen!

Action Item: Get Seen!

It's time to get strategic in order to gain visibility. Create a strategy in order to stay focused each quarter and amplify your visibility. Include the following in your strategy:

Focus: What is your primary focus?

Goal: What is your overarching goal?

Offer: What offer will you focus on?

Platform: Where will you spend the majority of your efforts?

Freebie: What opt in will you be promoting this quarter?

Chapter 10

Be the "Go-To" Expert

Goal: Build "know, like, and trust" through clear, concise messaging in order to move followers to a list you own by consistently providing massive value.

Now that you're gaining visibility with your ideal client, it's crucial to establish yourself as the go-to authority and position yourself as the solution to their problem, the next step in the journey to moving a follower to a buyer.

Clarity + Consistency = Conversions

Your messaging needs to be clear, consistent, and concise in order to attract aligned clients. If visibility is what gets you seen, then messaging is what really draws your ideal client into your world. Clear messaging raises your authority and positions your products or services as the obvious solution to the problem that your ideal client has. They can begin to see themselves as capable of achieving the results they desire when you show them the transformation from where they are to where they want to be.

This clarity enables you to create messaging that positions you as the authority because you understand your client inside out, speak their language, and address the mistakes and misconceptions holding them back. This doesn't require complexity; in fact, simplicity is key, and repetition becomes your ally. Yes, you might feel like a broken record, but the reality is that most people aren't paying close attention. With attention spans now shorter than a goldfish's, it takes over 20 interactions with a potential client before they're ready to buy.

When you take the time to clarify your messaging, your potential clients can self-diagnose that they NEED the solution you provide through your products or services. Consistently showing up not only demonstrates reliability but also builds trust with your audience. When your message isn't crystal clear, potential clients subconsciously question your authority to solve their problems.

Repetition not only establishes your authority but also positions you as the go-to specialist for the challenges your audience faces. This, in turn, facilitates referrals as others readily recognize you as the solution. Share content that prompts them to acknowledge their existing issues and guide them through the transformative process step by step.

Positioning yourself as the go-to solution for a specific problem may initially feel counterintuitive. However, consider it this way: if you broke your arm, would you consult your primary care physician? More likely, you'd seek an orthopedic specialist focusing on injuries like yours. And if you have an insurance co-pay, it's expected to be higher for a specialist than for a general practitioner. Why? Specialists command higher rates due to their expertise in a particular area. Clarity in your messaging showcases the value of your expertise.

By adopting a specialist mindset, you gain the ability to elevate your rates. It's about overcoming the scarcity mindset that leads you to think that helping everyone equates to better results. In reality, marketing to everyone leads to confusion among potential customers and clients, as no one understands what you do and how you do it.

Content Pillars

Content isn't limited to social media; it encompasses your website, email lists, podcasts, blog posts, speaking engagements, and more. Establishing content pillars is an approach that ensures that your message resonates across various platforms, reinforcing your position as the expert at solving a specific problem. Content pillars are three to five topics or themes aligned with the value you provide through your content.

When it comes to creating content, the possibilities are endless. Gone are the days of curated feeds filled with stock images. The key lies in identifying what resonates best with you and aligns with your ideal clients' preferences. Repetition and human connection emerge as the strategy that etches your brand into the memory of your audience, making you memorable and reliable. Your content does a number of things for your ideal client. It educates, empathizes, allows prospective clients to self-diagnose that they need the solution you provide, shows proof of concept through transformation and testimonials, and shares how you are different.

If a visitor lands on your page and encounters a mix of random posts showcasing your cat, a business tip, a workout, and random quotes, it leads to confusion, and they'll likely scroll past because it's not clear what you do. Embrace the feeling of being a broken record and stick to your content pillars to stay top of mind. This helps ensure that when they're ready to buy, you are the obvious choice. Your role is to be the reliable authority, like the always-there friend, not the one who only appears when they need something.

The Art of Listening

Are you a good listener? Most of us like to think we are, yet, oftentimes, we have become so distracted that we miss the answers we are searching so hard for. It turns out the answers are right in front of us if only we took the time to listen. For instance, when seeking content ideas, we commonly scroll through feeds of others in our industry.

What if, instead of scrolling and getting sucked into the trap of consumption, we actively listened in Facebook groups or engaged with our ideal clients' content, paying attention to their words? To truly understand your ideal client, you must think like them and incorporate the phrases you've gathered from your insights in Part One. Deliver what they truly need, not what you assume they need, through clear and concise content.

Once you've clarified your messaging, your content becomes a powerful sales tool. Ask questions to uncover their problems, guiding them toward your solution. Relate to and acknowledge their challenges. Your role is that of a problem solver; asking questions to clarify their needs helps you serve them effectively.

Often, our desire to talk overshadows the importance of listening. Talking may make us feel important, but true connection arises when we listen. Actively listening makes people feel seen and heard. To unveil their problems, encourage dialogue and attentively listen. The more they talk, the more problems surface, allowing you to position yourself as the solution. This not only enhances the value of your offer but also demonstrates how you save them time and money by solving their problems.

Audience versus Algorithm

Clients often blame the algorithm for their content struggles, but I urge you to shift your focus to your audience, not the algorithm. A great question to ask yourself is if you would engage with your content. Remember, your content is to serve your audience, not the algorithm.

The more value you provide, the smoother the sales process becomes. How? It's the law of reciprocity. By providing the knowledge they need to achieve a win, you build instant credibility, becoming the go-to problem solver in their minds. Satisfied clients refer you to others facing similar problems. You're creating content for your clients, not the algorithm.

If you're struggling to gain traction, assess if your content clearly reflects the problem you solve.

Problem-Awareness Content versus Value-Based Content

There are endless types of content you can create. I want to dive into two of the content types that are most important when you are looking to build authority, problem-awareness content and value-based content.

Problem-awareness content is a marketing concept which serves to make your ideal client conscious of a problem they have that they might not even be aware of. For instance, if I believe data is necessary for decision-making, I might create a post prompting you to consider whether you're tracking data in your business. You start to think, *Wait a minute, I'm not tracking any data* . . . should I be? What do I need to track? Why do I need to track it? As you ponder this, the realization dawns on you—maybe you have a problem that needs solving. Now that you are aware of the problem, I can seamlessly transition to the solution through value-based content.

You are attracting clients through your messaging, and when your messaging is off, you may find yourself with a following of unaligned followers versus ready buyers.

A common question I receive is, "How much should I give away for free?" Here's my perspective: all the information you provide is readily available, especially with the accessibility provided by technology, so give it all away for free. It may seem counterintuitive, but the more value you provide for free, the more authority and trust you build because you are providing a taste of the experience they will receive. If you have trouble wrapping your mind around this concept, think of it this way. You could hear Taylor Swift on the radio, watch a prerecorded concert at a movie theater, or invest in a ticket to her live performance. The music is the same, but the experience differs with the option you choose, and the price you're willing to pay increases exponentially with the perceived value of each experience.

Quick Content Audit

I audit my content regularly to see if I'm clear in my messaging by asking myself the following questions:

- Does my content clearly highlight the value of my offer?
- Does my content show the transformation/results that a client can expect?
- Does it address their needs, desires, challenges, and objections?
- Looking at my social media content, is it obvious what I do and how?
- Is it obvious how my offer is different from others?

The key is to identify what resonates most with your audience. Dive into your analytics to gain valuable insights: observe which emails have the highest open rates, take note of saved and shared content, and pay attention to what generates the most engagement. The answers you seek are readily available—you just need to invest the time to uncover them.

Moving to a List You Own

Frequently, social media takes center stage in most businesses' marketing strategies. The belief that success is directly tied to follower counts and shiny metrics has been ingrained in us. However, it's critical to reassess our relationship with social media. Followers don't automatically translate to buyers, so it's time to shift the focus away from stressing over follower numbers and concentrate on serving those already in your world. Utilize social media as a tool to guide potential customers to a list you own, such as an email list.

It's essential to recognize that you don't own your social media accounts or the content you share on them. These platforms can shut down your account at any time, for any reason. I've witnessed this happen numerous times. After investing countless hours in creating amazing content, you could lose it all overnight and find yourself back at square one. The saving grace lies in a list you own. Your email list can be used in a variety of ways, including building relationships, sharing value, and keeping you top of mind. We'll go into more detail on this in the next chapter. But the question arises: how do you transition followers from social media to your email list?

The most straightforward method is through an opt-in or freebie. Create something of significant value, juicy enough that your potential client would willingly pay for it. Offer them a quick win to give them a taste of the transformation you provide. The more value you provide, the more authority you gain in their eyes. This could take the form of a webinar, a free PDF checklist, a guide, an e-book, or a private podcast stream—there are endless possibilities. Prospective clients provide their email address through an opt-in form, and you reciprocate with the value they seek. Set up a landing page with automation to have the information sent directly to them, and voilà—a new name on your list.

Share this opt-in everywhere, including social media, which serves as an excellent platform to promote your free offers and opt-ins, enticing your ideal clients onto a list that you own. In addition, share it in the variety of opportunities we outlined in Chapter 9. Use a clear call to action (CTA) in your content to drive ideal clients to this opt-in to bring your followers into your world.

Staying Consistent

Consistency can be a challenge, especially when it feels like nobody is paying attention. Yet, the truth is, no one makes a purchase decision based on a single post. Rest assured, people are consuming your information even when they don't engage. I've had numerous clients emerge seemingly out of nowhere, never having interacted with my content. Trust is built through consistency, not sporadic appearances. Instead of fixating on numbers, concentrate on crafting exceptional content for that one person you can genuinely impact. Once you connect with one, you'll find more who resonate with your message and mission.

Action Item: A Day in the Life

If you're finding it challenging to create content for your ideal client, a great way to do this is to perform a simple exercise developed by Fran Johnson of Loughborough University, England called "Day in the Life of…" Think about what your ideal clients are going through from the minute they wake up until the minute they go to sleep. What are their challenges, habits, behaviors? What makes them tick? When you know exactly what they're doing and where they are spending their time, you can use this as content that meets them right where they are—content that gets it in their head that, *yes, she totally gets what I am going through right now.*

Chapter 11
Building Relationship Capital

Goal: Convert prospective clients into buyers by building relationships.

People Buy from People

All too often as business owners, we get stuck in the cycle of "more." We think we need more followers, more platforms, more strategies, more everything, in order to grow our business. I get it because I have totally been there too. We've been sold on the idea that a bigger audience equals more sales. Yes, an audience is important; however, cultivating the right audience is far more important. I would much rather have 100 followers that are my ideal buyers versus 1,000 random followers that are not my ideal clients. The pursuit of "more" often blinds us to the value of those already present in our world.

Think about it this way. You receive an invitation to a highly anticipated gathering—an event that promises excitement and value, much like your opt-in offer. Enthusiastically, you decide to attend. Yet, upon arriving, you realize that the host, instead of engaging with the present guests, completely ignores everyone and abruptly exits the venue. Their sole focus is on finding more people to invite to the party. Now, reflect on how this situation would make you feel. The disappointment and lack of attention certainly don't foster trust or a sense of value, do they?

When someone enters your world, how are you nurturing them and building a relationship with them? Are you taking the time to say hi and acknowledge their presence? Have you taken the time to connect with those on your email list, your followers on social media, everyone in your Facebook group, all of your connections on LinkedIn? The real magic happens when you nurture and build a relationship with those who have opted in to you. As humans, we crave connection. We want to feel seen and appreciated. Taking the time to connect makes you even more likable and sets you apart from the competition because you have taken the time to show that you care. It goes beyond a mere transaction; it's about showing that you genuinely care. This simple act often sparks meaningful conversations, and as we know, conversations are the key to turning leads into conversions.

It's essential to recognize that this is not the appropriate time to present a paid offer—an immediate turnoff, much like a random stranger proposing marriage on the street. When nurturing prospective clients, the key is to focus on serving rather than selling. Your new follower or subscriber has expressed interest in your content and willingly joined your community to discover more about who you are and what your values are.

Establishing a strong relationship with your potential clients builds trust. Show genuine interest in their needs, actively listen to their concerns, and tailor your offering to align with their specific requirements because you have their best interests in mind. Establishing a relationship based on trust and understanding can help diminish self-doubt, as clients feel more comfortable expressing their concerns.

Stop worrying about unfollows and unsubscribes; these actions mean nothing about you. Not everyone will resonate with your message, and that's perfectly fine—your message isn't meant for everyone. Those who stick around are typically interested in what you have to say. Moreover, unfollows and unsubscribes offer valuable data to pinpoint messaging gaps in your content. Strive to build a following filled with potential buyers, not a collection of bots and disinterested followers.

Engaging your followers through polls and encouraging replies to your email campaigns are excellent strategies for building relationships and creating a sense of community. By asking for their opinions and feedback, you not only show that you value their input but also involve them in the decision-making process. This tactic goes beyond serving your audience; it makes them feel like an integral part of your community. I've personally experienced the power of this approach when planning an entire event with the help of my followers. From choosing the date to deciding on colors and themes, every step involved their input through polls, making the event a collaborative effort that everyone felt connected to.

The value of relationship capital can't be overstated in business growth. Thriving businesses are built on authentic relationships. Simply being genuine and human in your interactions with a mindset of service can lead to more sales in a way that feels genuine rather than spammy. Remember, if someone is already part of your world, they've willingly opted in, indicating their interest in what you have to offer. It's all about nurturing those connections with authenticity and providing content to serve rather than to sell.

Leveraging Email to Nurture

Email marketing is a powerful platform for building meaningful connections based on shared values and interests and for nurturing relationships. It boasts an average ROI of 42 percent, surpassing many other marketing strategies. An email list is a list that you own. It provides valuable insights into who is engaging with your content, granting you valuable data for strategic decisions.

Beyond metrics, email marketing positions you top of mind. Even if someone isn't ready to invest in your products or services yet, your consistent appearances in their inbox remind them that you're there when they need you. Even non-openers retain a subtle reminder that you offer a solution to their problems.

Email marketing goes beyond promotions; it's a tool to humanize your brand, especially in an era where people increasingly prefer to buy from other people versus massive brands. In a world longing for connection, embracing your authenticity becomes a selling point. Your relatability, personal story, and vulnerability deepen the connection, enabling you to stand out even more. Keep in mind that showing up imperfectly is far more impactful than not showing up at all. Consistency lays the groundwork for enduring relationships.

If the thought of creating more content makes you sick to your stomach, consider designing emails around your content pillars. Use this long-form content to repurpose in the form of social media content. As we discussed earlier, consistency is key. Stick to your brand pillars, share compelling stories, and provide value; avoid the constant hard pitch. Hard selling in every email can be off-putting, and remember, we're aiming to be the reliable friend, not the one who only shows up when they need something. In my emails, I create a space for my subscribers to share their thoughts by encouraging replies. This dual-purpose strategy not only strengthens the "know, like, and trust" factor by building relationships but also positively impacts email deliverability.

Speaking of deliverability, the spam folder is a real concern. To steer clear of it, various strategies exist. Watch out for words and phrases that could trigger email providers to send you directly to the spam folder such as "free," "buy," and "urgent," to name a few. Additionally, regularly clearing out inactive subscribers and managing a low bounce rate (emails that don't get delivered) is crucial to maintain a positive email sender reputation and avoid being marked as spam.

Bonus tip: regularly back up your list to a CSV file to safeguard against unforeseen events.

Leveraging email analytics is a powerful strategy to identify your warm audience—those opening and clicking your emails. Delve into the data, use it to your advantage, and take the opportunity to further nurture these prospective clients on social media. Initiate meaningful conversations and engage with their content. Remember, this engagement on social media isn't about selling; it's about establishing authentic connections. While it does require time and effort, the payoff is attracting aligned clients because your content is doing the selling for you.

Learn from My Experience

List size can quickly become another shiny object. Last year, I leaned into participating in free summits and bundles as a visibility tactic. While this strategy significantly increased my email list size, analyzing the data revealed that the leads weren't qualified. Recognizing this allowed me to understand that it wasn't a personal issue but rather the challenge of an unaligned audience. Tracking such data empowered me to make informed decisions, emphasizing the importance of being selective in choosing opportunities to participate in and ensuring alignment with my target audience.

You Can Control This

Prospects are analyzing you, both consciously and subconsciously, as they consider questions such as "Do I genuinely like you? Are you attentive to my needs? Do you make me feel valued and significant? Do you comprehend my challenges and concerns? Can I trust you, believing that you hold the key to solving the problems I'm facing?" Ultimately, people make purchases because you've succeeded in making them feel acknowledged and understood, creating a sense of security by offering the solution they've been seeking. When a prospective client feels that you truly "get" them, understand their situation, and possess the remedy to their issues, it establishes a profound connection that leads to trust and, ultimately, a decision to invest in your solution.

The timing of a purchase is beyond your control, but the efforts invested in providing value, consistent presence, and relationship building eventually yield results. Your skills capture attention, your service generates interest, and the personal connection you establish leads to conversions. At the core of effective sales is the art of building relationships and embracing your authenticity. It's likely that there are numerous individuals who have already shown interest in you, yet you may not have taken the time to acknowledge them. Channel your focus into connecting with those already in your world.

While nurturing relationships demands time and energy, a strategic approach ensures that your content continues to serve as a powerful sales tool. A warm audience comprised of the right buyers is essential for successful sales, and those who have opted into your world represent this warm audience. Recognize their micro-commitment to you and dedicate yourself to nurturing these relationships. Make them feel seen, heard, valued, and appreciated by connecting with them and demonstrating your understanding of their challenges. In the end, people are more concerned with how you can help them rather than the number of certifications you hold.

Action Item: Email Marketing

If you haven't taken the time to pop into your email list's inboxes lately, it's time to start. Remember, you are writing an email, not a novel. Don't overcomplicate it. Repurpose a post you did, share a life update, be a human, and start to position yourself as top of mind.

Chapter 12

Sales = Solution

Goal: Provide clients with the transformation that they want and, in turn, you get what you want, a.k.a. money.

The word "sales" often conjures images of the stereotypical sleazy used car salesman or the overly eager furniture salespeople who pounce the moment we step into a store. To achieve the financial success you desire, it's crucial to examine your relationship with money. Consider how you perceive money and wealth by reflecting on the stories you tell yourself about money and the narratives you might have inherited from your upbringing. Understanding and reshaping these money-related beliefs can significantly impact your approach to sales and financial success.

Our underlying beliefs about money can hold us back from sharing our solutions. Money, in its essence, is a tool—a conduit for creating more impact. Shifting our perspective, we realize that the more we generate, the more significant our impact becomes. It's a transformative realization, linking financial success not just to personal gain but to the power of making a positive difference.

Every belief about money is a choice, and you have the power to choose. Examining the stories we tell ourselves, whether limiting or empowering, allows us to reshape our narrative. Money goes beyond a transactional entity; it serves as a catalyst for change. If you're struggling to reframe your money mindset, create a list of how the money you make can be used to create a positive impact in the world.

The world needs more individuals who use their wealth for good. As you navigate your financial journey, embrace self-awareness, make choices aligned with your values, and take responsibility for the narratives you carry. The pursuit of financial success isn't just a destination; it's a journey of self-discovery and empowerment.

Sales doesn't have to feel sleazy; instead, it requires strategy. At its core, sales is about presenting a solution—an invitation to address someone's problem. By demonstrating the value of the solution, you create an equal energy exchange where, if the prospective client sees the value, they reciprocate with something in return, typically money.

The preceding steps are necessary because they lay the groundwork for a successful sales process. Having a well-thought-out plan allows you to leverage your time and energy effectively to transition followers into buyers. Attempting to sell without warming up your audience through the preceding steps can result in a lower conversion rate.

Why We Buy

A consistent and strategic presence is key because the business landscape is noisy, and people aren't paying as much attention as we may assume. It's essential to overcome the assumption that people already know what you offer. Your job is to consistently show up and present the solution to your warm leads. Converting someone through a cold message is highly unlikely, but presenting an invitation to someone who knows, likes, and trusts you makes the process smoother. This underscores the importance of tracking data, as discussed in Part Two.

To ensure a successful sales strategy, it's critical to have a sales plan in place and start with the end in mind. Reverse engineering your sales goals allows you to approach sales from a place of abundance, understanding the natural ebbs and flows in your business. Analyzing data provides insights to plan accordingly, helping you navigate cash flow fluctuations throughout the year. Sales, fundamentally, is about presenting the right offer to the right audience, with the right message, at the right time.

Before a customer makes a purchase, several factors must align. First, they must perceive your product or service as the solution to a significant problem they want to address, and the consequences of not solving this issue have become too great to ignore. Second, they need to feel secure investing money in your offering, trusting it to resolve their problem and deliver the desired results. Purchases don't happen when there's no need, no financial capacity, no urgency, no desire, and no trust.

Understanding that people buy to fulfill their needs is essential. They encounter a problem, can afford your solution, have the decision-making ability, and find your offering as the solution to their problem. Your role is to bridge the gap, guiding potential clients to perceive your product or service as the answer to their specific issue. Consistently showcasing your solution to a warm audience reinforces this perception. When you focus on delivering tangible results and present an invitation to those actively seeking your solution, you effectively justify the value of the transformation. Most purchases are driven by the desire to save time, alleviate pain, or increase financial resources. Emotion prompts the initial purchase, with logic serving to rationalize the decision.

Often, a lack of sales has little to do with the quality of your product or service. Even if you offer the best on the market, the key is selling customers what they believe they need (their desired result) while providing them with what they actually need to achieve the desired result. In my experience working with clients, I've observed many individuals playing small and hesitating to sell because of a fear of rejection. However, it's crucial to recognize that the answer will always be no if you don't ask. Fear of rejection often stems from a deep-rooted desire for acceptance and self-protection, causing missed opportunities.

It's time to stop assuming that you're a bother, abandon self-limiting stories, and start asking for the sale. Embrace boldness and courage. Selling, like any skill, becomes easier with practice. Reframe the idea of a no as a "next opportunity" because, more often than not, rejection is a form of protection. When making an ask, we tend to focus on ourselves, while the person receiving the request is often more concerned about the difficulty of saying no. Human nature is to help others, and the fear of rejection triggers the fight-or-flight response. By overcoming your attachment to outcomes and viewing rejection as an opportunity for growth, you can seize more chances to be bold and open the doors to success.

Your Value Proposition

Your value proposition is the tangible value you bring to your clients, saving them time, money, energy, and resources. People pay for solutions to their problems, and positioning yourself as the best value for the solution is fundamental to your success. Clearly articulate the ROI of your solution, emphasizing the transformative journey from their current state to where they want to be. Your unique combination of experiences, knowledge, and beliefs is what sets you apart.

Remember the Taylor Swift concert analogy we discussed in Chapter 10? Pricing strategy is all about perceived value. Your goal is to position yourself so that the value you provide far outweighs the price you charge. If someone truly desires your offering, they will find the means to pay for it because they recognize and value what you bring to the table. The goal is to position yourself in a way that the value you provide supports the price you are charging.

Pain Point Marketing Versus Desire Marketing

There are many trains of thought as to whether pain point marketing or desire marketing strategies are more effective. I've found it often depends on what resonates best with your ideal clients. Research indicates that approximately 75 percent of purchases are motivated by a desire to move away from pain, as problems drive the need for change. Clients seek solutions, and for them to commit, they must believe that the change is worth it and feel a sense of safety in taking that risk.

While emphasizing pain points is effective, it's equally crucial to paint a vivid picture of the desired outcome. Incorporating a mix of content that bridges the gap between the current state (pain) and the desired state (pleasure) is key. Focus less on the intricate features and more on the overarching benefits. Make your clients feel understood and assure them that you can effectively solve their problems. The foundation laid in clarifying your messaging in Part One provides you with all the necessary information to help you identify their current state, present a vision with the problem solved, and outline the steps for them to reach that desired state.

Navigating Objections

I used to dread objections, but I've come to appreciate them as my potential clients' way of seeking the additional information they need to make an informed decision. When they pose questions or express concerns, it's a sign of genuine interest in what I'm offering. Instead of trying to convince them, which often stems from a scarcity mindset,

I approach objections with curiosity. I put myself in their shoes, asking questions to understand their perspective better. My goal is to provide the information they seek, anchoring it back to their desired state. In doing so, I aim to extend an invitation to the solution that addresses their specific challenges. After all, sales is about facilitating a decision-making process that aligns with the best interests of my prospective clients.

Objections arise for a variety of reasons. Prospective clients might have experienced setbacks in the past, faced challenges with other methods, or be dealing with undisclosed factors. Taking the time to cultivate a relationship, asking thoughtful questions, and actively listening become essential in this process. Once you've created a safe space through attentive listening and truly understanding the root cause of their problems, clients often reveal the answers needed to position your solution effectively. It's crucial to delve into their problems, understand the impact, and uncover the reasons for their struggles. Ultimately, we possess the solution to guide them toward the transformation they desire—a journey that they recognize as valuable in terms of both time and money.

When we break down the multitude of objections that we could potentially receive, we can generalize most objections into four main categories: price, spouse, time, and belief. Let's break each of them down.

Price Objection: This objection arises when the prospect perceives your product or service as too expensive.

Strategies to overcome the objection:

- o Value demonstration: Clearly communicate the value of the transformation that you provide and the benefits they will receive in relation to the investment. Share case studies, testimonials, or examples that showcase the positive outcomes and successes your previous clients have achieved. This social proof can instill confidence in the value you bring, making the price seem more reasonable.
- o Payment plans: Offer flexible payment options or installment plans, if that feels aligned to you, or consider extending an invitation to another product or service in your product suite which requires less of an investment.
- o Comparison: Showcase how your product or service compares favorably to alternatives in terms of cost-effectiveness. Demonstrate the ROI that clients can expect from your product or service by explaining how your offering will save them money, time, or resources in the long run, making it a worthwhile investment.

Spouse Objection: The prospect may express the need to consult with or get approval from their spouse or partner before making a purchase. This situation commonly occurs in significant financial decisions, long-term commitments, or purchases that may impact the household. Spouses may have concerns about the cost, necessity, or value of the product or service, and they want to be involved in the decision-making process.

Strategies to overcome the objection:

o Involvement: Encourage them to involve their spouse in the decision-making process. Recognize that decisions involving spouses may take time. Be patient, understanding, and supportive throughout the process. Avoid applying pressure, and instead, focus on building trust.

o Provide information: Offer materials or resources that they can share with their spouse.

o Follow-up: Agree on a suitable time for a follow-up discussion that includes both parties. This allows you to address concerns directly and ensures that everyone involved has a clear understanding of the offering.

I have found that prospective clients use their spouse as an objection when, in reality, they haven't even asked their spouse. More often than not, the spouse is extremely supportive and encouraging of their decision; however, the prospective client has created a narrative that they are not worthy of the investment, so they won't even ask and assume their spouse will say no.

Time Objection: This objection stems from a perceived lack of time to commit to your product or service.

Strategies to overcome the objection:

o Highlight efficiency: Emphasize the time-saving benefits of your offering. Showcase how your offering can provide immediate benefits and potential consequences of delaying the decision. Showcase how your product or service can deliver immediate benefits or solve urgent issues. If clients can see quick results, they may be more inclined to make time for the solution.

o   Flexibility: Whether it's automation, streamlined processes, or quick implementation, make it clear how your offering can fit seamlessly into their schedule.

o   Prioritization: Help them see the value of prioritizing your solution amid their busy schedule. Break down the steps and timelines, showing that the process won't be overly burdensome and can be accommodated within their existing schedule.

Belief Objection: This objection, often deeply rooted in self-doubt and fear of success, can manifest as an underlying sales objection when potential clients question their own ability to successfully implement or benefit from your product or service. It often stems from uncertainties, fear of failure, or concerns about whether they are making the right decision.

Strategies to overcome the objection:

o   Understand and acknowledge concerns: Begin by understanding and acknowledging the specific concerns or doubts your potential client may have. This demonstrates empathy and opens the door for effective communication.

o Provide evidence: Share testimonials, case studies, or success stories so that they can build confidence in themselves and picture themselves in the transformation of others. Real-world examples can serve as powerful reassurance.

o Education: Offer additional information or resources to proactively address any potential challenges or obstacles that clients might face during the implementation process. By acknowledging and offering solutions to potential issues, you demonstrate transparency and preparedness.

o Encourage questions and communication: Encourage open communication and invite clients to ask questions. Responding promptly and thoroughly to their inquiries helps build trust and dispel doubts.

At the end of the day, it's important to identify if the raised objection is the sole limiting factor preventing them from an investment in your services. Don't make assumptions about the specific barrier standing between you and the sale. Understanding objections at a deeper level creates an atmosphere of trust during the decision-making process.

The Power of Silence

It's important to recognize the power of strategic silence throughout the conversation. Offering prospects the space to reflect and process the information we've discussed is essential. This purposeful pause provides them a moment to process details, consider their needs, and formulate questions or responses.

There is a common tendency in conversations with prospective clients to fill the silence with chatter, especially when driven by a sense of scarcity. Talking excessively in these moments can be misconstrued as desperation, potentially putting off potential buyers. Silence creates a space that prompts the client to fill it. This encourages them to actively participate in the conversation, share more information, and express their thoughts or concerns.

In addition, leveraging silence during a conversation demonstrates the salesperson's confidence in their product or service. It indicates that they are not rushing the client and are secure in the value of what they are offering. Sales professionals who embrace silence are often better active listeners. Active listening strategies allow us to pay attention to the client's verbal and non-verbal cues, giving us valuable insights into the client's mindset.

Communication Is Key

Awareness of potential objections enhances communication with potential clients. It enables you to tailor your messaging to address specific concerns, making your pitch more compelling and relevant to the individual needs and hesitations of your audience. When you address objections head-on, it builds trust with your audience. It shows that you are transparent, attentive to their concerns, and committed to finding solutions that meet their needs. By addressing objections early, you streamline the decision-making process. Potential clients are more likely to move forward with a purchase when their concerns have been acknowledged and resolved, reducing hesitation and delays. In some cases, objections may arise due to misunderstandings or lack of information.

Remember, sales is about presenting prospective clients with a solution to the problem they have. Trying to convince someone to choose you is exhausting and stems from a place of scarcity. Through your content, present potential objections as a way to address them even before you have a conversation with a prospective client. The goal is to have informed buyers. It is their job to determine whether they want to accept your invitation.

Fortune in the Follow-Up

A significant portion of sales, approximately 20 to 30 percent, occurs during the follow-up process rather than at the initial offer. Life is unpredictable, and people get busy. The act of following up demonstrates that you genuinely care. Remember, it's not your responsibility to determine whether it's a definitive no. Some clients may need more time to decide that your solution is the right fit for their problem. When a client declines your invitation, it doesn't equate to a rejection of you personally; often, it's a lack of sufficient information to say yes.

Taking the extra step to follow up is a practice that sets you apart. Many individuals may face distractions or challenges that push decisions to the back burner. By consistently following up with prospective clients, you show that you care about their needs and are committed to providing the information or support required for them to make an informed decision. This dedication to thorough communication not only sets you apart from others but also increases the likelihood of closing deals in the follow-up stage.

If a prospect does not commit to an investment in the service I provide, I ask for their permission to follow up on a specific date. Why ask for permission?

Seeking permission demonstrates respect for the prospective client's time and their decision-making process. It acknowledges that their time is valuable, and you are considerate of their preferences. This helps to avoid any perception of unsolicited or intrusive follow-ups, fostering a more positive interaction. Asking for permission to follow up opens the door for the prospective client to provide feedback or share specific reasons for their decision. This feedback can be valuable for understanding their concerns, objections, or questions that arose following the call.

Most importantly, asking for permission builds trust by allowing the prospective client to feel in control of the communication process. Trust is a crucial element in any business relationship, and respectful communication contributes to trustworthiness by showing that your priority is to meet the client's needs and preferences. Focusing on building a connection, rather than pressuring for an immediate sale, sets the stage for a continued relationship, even if the prospect doesn't convert immediately.

When Nothing Is Working

I know it's tempting to burn it all down and start from scratch when nothing seems to be working.

Allow yourself to get curious and reflect on your answers to the following questions:

- Are those consuming my content ideal clients?
- Have I taken the time to engage with them, build relationships, and listen to them?
- Am I meeting my clients exactly where they are, listening to their challenges, and addressing their needs in my content?
- How am I getting in front of my ideal clients and expanding my reach?
- Is my messaging clear, highlighting the value of the transformation that I provide?
- Do those in my world know what I offer and how to buy from me?
- Am I consistently showing up as the solution to their problems?
- Am I adhering to my daily nonnegotiables and showing up consistently to provide value and position myself as the expert in my space?
- How often am I showing up and presenting an invitation to the solution I provide?
- Am I taking the time to follow up with leads?

- Am I addressing potential objections and concerns in my content?

Sales is a skill, and it's a skill that takes time to develop. The reality of owning a business is that there are ups and downs. Instead of recreating everything from the ground up every time you hit a rough patch, remember to leverage the data you have gathered.

Action Item: Identify Objections

List your most common sales objections and start to address these in your content. Staying ahead of potential objections will help you navigate the sales process with ease.

Chapter 13

Creating Raving Fans

Goal: Let your customers be your best salespeople.

As we discussed earlier, it's not always about chasing more prospective clients or customers. Oftentimes, there is endless opportunity hiding in plain sight in what I refer to as the three *R*'s: relationships, retention, and referrals. Strategically leveraging these three pillars has grown my business exponentially.

Relationships

Relationship capital is commonly undervalued. I encourage you to refer back to Chapter 4, where we discuss how to effectively utilize networking and collaboration opportunities as a strategy to build relationships with fellow entrepreneurs.

Whether it's a user-friendly website, an easy checkout process, or hassle-free returns, prioritize convenience to enhance your clients' overall experience. Actively seek opportunities to stand out. Exceptional customer experiences set a business apart from competitors. In industries where products or services are similar, a positive customer experience becomes a significant differentiator.

At the end of the day, taking the time to go the extra mile will strengthen your relationships with your clients, improve their overall experience, and in turn, create raving fans who will remain loyal to your brand. These loyal clients willingly promote your business, defend it in the face of criticism, and contribute to a positive brand image.

A loyal customer base can provide stability during market fluctuations. Strong relationships make it easier to introduce new products, services, or changes, as customers are more likely to embrace them.

Retention

We're trying to work smarter not harder, right? One of the easiest ways to save energy is through customer retention. It is far easier to sell to someone who has already purchased something from you and had a phenomenal experience than to a new lead. The sales cycle is exponentially shorter when selling to those who have already bought from you. They already know, like, and trust you because you delivered a high-quality experience and results that solved their problem, so they are likely to become repeat customers. It's important that you have a plan in place to keep in touch with customers after they have bought from you and continue to nurture these relationships.

Harvard Business Review reported that increasing customer retention rates by 5 percent increases profits by 25 to 95 percent.[6] It's often more cost-effective to retain existing customers than to acquire new ones, and existing customers contribute to a stable and predictable revenue stream. The study also mentions that the success rate of selling to an existing customer is 60 to 70 percent, while the success rate of selling to a new customer is 5 to 20 percent. Satisfied customers are inclined to make repeat purchases, resulting in a higher customer lifetime value to the business. This is why loyalty programs have been so successful in the mass retail market. Treat your current customers like GOLD.

How do you make yourself stand out so you have a loyal group of customers? It starts with exceptional customer service, which helps you build trust and shows that you prioritize their satisfaction. Keep customers informed about order status, delays, or any relevant information. Solve issues promptly, showing that you genuinely care about their satisfaction.

Using the SOPs that we established in Part Two, look at ways you can make your customers feel valued and appreciated by delivering a high-level experience. They have invested in you, so you want to show them how much you appreciate them. Take the time to check in regularly with your current and past clients, listen to their needs, and celebrate their wins. Their

6. Amy Gallo, "The Value of Keeping the Right Customers," *Harvard Business Review*, October 29, 2014, https://hbr.org/2014/10/the-value-of-keeping-the-right-customers.

success is your success. A satisfied customer is more likely to leave you an awesome testimonial or send you a great referral (we'll dive into referrals shortly).

Looking for ways to go above and beyond with your clients? Here are a few ideas to get you started.

- Send a handwritten note with their order or to celebrate a win with them.
- Celebrate important milestones in your customers' lives, whether it's a birthday, anniversary, or other significant event by sending a card.
- Surprise customers with unexpected gestures or gifts. This could be an onboarding gift, a program completion gift, a discount on their birthday, a free sample, or a special offer exclusive to loyal customers.
- Occasionally surprise customers by including small, branded merchandise like stickers, tote bags, or other small items in their orders.
- Collaborate with other brands to offer exclusive partnership discounts to your customers, expanding the value they receive.
- Host special events or sales dedicated to showing appreciation for your customers, such as an annual customer appreciation day, flash sales, or early access to new product launches.

In order to retain customers, under promise and over deliver.

Referrals and Reviews

Referrals and word-of-mouth advertising are one of the most powerful, cost-effective, yet frequently overlooked marketing avenues in business. Satisfied clients who have gotten great results help you organically grow your business by becoming advocates for your brand. They're also referral sources who send you other aligned customers.

We are heavily influenced by those around us, and with the endless choices available, we tend to ask our friends for recommendations since we trust them and know they have our best interests at heart. A recommendation from a friend implies a personal endorsement. When a friend recommends someone to us, we are even more likely to choose that product or service. It's much more persuasive than just picking a random name off the Internet or social media.

Let's use an example. I had a great experience with a graphic designer recommended by a friend. I looked at her work and loved who she was as a person on social media. But, because she was recommended by a friend, I saw the value and quickly invested in her services. Yes, there are a million graphic designers out there, but I chose her because of the recommendation, and now I refer her all the time to those who would find her services valuable. Referrals are targeted marketing to an interested audience without any extra marketing effort on your end.

Referrals can help expand your business's reach beyond your immediate network. As satisfied customers share their positive experiences, your business gains exposure to a broader audience, potentially reaching individuals who might not have come across your offerings through traditional marketing channels.

Leads generated through word of mouth often have higher conversion rates. Since they come with a recommendation from someone the potential customer knows and trusts, they are more likely to convert into actual customers.

Positive word of mouth contributes to the creation of a supportive community around your brand. As more people share their experiences, a sense of community and shared interest can develop, fostering customer loyalty and long-term engagement.

Word of mouth provides an ongoing feedback loop for your business. It allows you to understand what aspects of your products or services are resonating positively with customers and what areas might need improvement. This feedback is valuable for refining your offerings.

Businesses that consistently receive positive word-of-mouth referrals gain a competitive advantage. Positive reviews and recommendations set your business apart from competitors and can influence potential customers who are comparing different options in the market.

You can implement a referral program or brand ambassador program that rewards clients for referring new business. This could include discounts, exclusive access, or other incentives.

This facilitates organic growth by tapping into the social circles of existing clients. Affiliate marketing programs give a percentage of each sale to the referral source. These programs reward successful referrals and motivate current and past clients to actively advocate for the business.

There are countless ways to get referrals and reviews. It simply comes down to doing what feels good to you and making the ask. Be specific about the kind of referrals you are looking for, and explain how their recommendation would be valuable.

Ask those who had a great experience with you to leave a review on Google—remember, this helps with search ability for locally based businesses. You can incentivize them with a small gift, such as a cup of coffee, in exchange for a review to create an equal energy exchange. Make the process easy by providing a direct link to your preferred platform or a conversation starter to help them create their review. The most effective time to ask is right after they have had a positive experience or a win in using your product or service.

Reviews Matter

When you are looking to buy something, you want to make sure you're getting your money's worth. If it's a product or service that you don't often use, it has a high price tag, or it's something you haven't purchased before, you will most likely look at the reviews.

Positive reviews from real customers build trust among potential buyers and create credibility for the business.

Consumers are more likely to trust the opinions of fellow consumers than promotional messages from the business. Reviews can influence the decision-making process, as prospective customers often read reviews to understand the experiences of others before making a purchase decision.

Positive reviews serve as social proof and add a human touch to your brand, indicating that others have had a positive experience with the business. They provide stories and experiences from real people, making the business more relatable and creating a connection with potential customers. This reassures potential customers by showing that the business values customer feedback and is responsive to concerns. Reviews validate the quality of the products or services, which becomes a competitive advantage and a reason for customers to choose it over others.

Navigating the Negative

No matter how incredible your product or service is, you aren't going to be for everyone, and the more you grow, the greater the potential to receive a negative review. This can feel completely devastating for a business owner, but everyone is entitled to their own opinion. Unfortunately, there are individuals out there who troll the online space looking to create havoc.

The way you handle negative reviews can influence the perception of potential customers. Demonstrating a commitment to resolving issues and improving your business based on feedback can turn a negative situation into a positive one. When you encounter a negative review, the following will help you effectively navigate the process.

- Stay calm and objective.

Negative reviews can be emotional, but it's crucial to respond promptly, calmly, and objectively to show that you care about the feedback. Avoid reacting defensively or emotionally. This is someone's opinion and, although it can feel personal, their opinion is just that—an opinion. It is not a reflection of your worth as a human. Take a deep breath and take time to assess the situation before responding.

- Acknowledge the issue.

In acknowledging the customer's concerns, you're demonstrating empathy and understanding. Let them know that you appreciate their feedback and take their concerns seriously.

- Apologize and take responsibility.

Apologize for any inconvenience or negative experience the customer may have had. Taking responsibility demonstrates accountability and a commitment to resolving the issue.

- Move the conversation offline.

While addressing the issue publicly is essential, encourage the customer to continue the conversation offline. Provide contact details or a customer support email where they can discuss the matter in more detail. Even if it is something that was completely out of your hands, saying "you're right" can quickly de-escalate a confrontation with an unhappy customer. Encourage them to vent and let it all out while you listen.

- Provide a solution or explanation.

Offer a practical solution to address the customer's concerns and ask them what would "make things right." This could involve a replacement, a refund, or additional support. If the issue is more complex, provide a clear explanation of the situation.

- Learn from feedback.

Negative reviews can offer valuable insights into areas where your business can improve. Use this feedback constructively to enhance your products, services, or customer experience. After addressing the issue, encourage the customer to share their updated experience. Positive follow-up reviews can help mitigate the impact of the initial negative feedback.

Navigating this process can be an emotional roller coaster. Throughout the interactions with a dissatisfied client, always maintain a professional tone. Avoid engaging in arguments or responding defensively. Your response reflects your brand's image, and professionalism is key. In some cases, negative reviews may cross legal boundaries with false statements or defamation. If you believe a review violates legal standards, seek legal advice on the appropriate course of action.

In leveraging the power of relationships, retention, and referrals, consistently providing excellent service and authentically expressing your gratitude, you can create an environment where clients feel motivated to refer others and share their positive experiences.

Mapping out your customer journey and sales process can seem daunting. However, taking the time to work through your customer journey will pay you back tenfold.

Action Item: Map It Out

Map out your customer journey from start to finish. Here's an overview of the framework to get you started:

Visibility: create awareness and attract ideal clients.

Authority: build "know, like, and trust" with ideal clients through clear messaging in order to move to a list you own.

Nurture: build relationships with ideal clients who have opted in.

Sell: demonstrate the value of your product or service and present the custom solution to a problem.

Customer Experience: let your customers be your best salespeople by focusing on retention and referrals.

Part Four: The Missing Piece of the Puzzle The Exact Formula for Success

Chapter 14

Getting the Results You Want

Starting a Business Is Easy . . . or Is It?

Starting a business is now easier than ever. Gone are the days when we had to go to the library, dig through the card catalog, search the encyclopedias, and spend tens of thousands on college courses that didn't actually give us the practical, real-world tactics we needed to grow a business in a constantly evolving digital landscape.

The wealth of knowledge and resources needed to build a business from the ground up are now just a Google search away. The information that will guide you step by step to achieving the success you desire is readily available in the form of YouTube videos, podcasts, online courses, mentors at every turn, and entire platforms dedicated to connecting people and marketing your business for free. Harvard Business School offers select business courses to the general public for free, and LinkedIn Learning has an incredible library of thousands of free courses teaching you business strategy.

Despite the abundance of information, the reality is that only 6 percent of businesses reach the six-figure mark. While social media showcases a narrative of widespread success with businesses hitting six figures and achieving 10K months as the norm, the truth is more complex. Many aspiring entrepreneurs, observing others' apparent success, believe that there must be a hidden secret waiting to be uncovered in the next high-ticket course, free webinar, or podcast.

While strategy is essential and can be laid out step by step, it is just one piece of the puzzle. Building a thriving business requires more than strategy. Are you ready to dive in? Let's go.

A Consumptivitis Culture

In the "on-demand" society we live in, we've developed an addiction to consuming information. Consuming is a passive activity, easier than actually taking action, that doesn't involve the level of critical thinking that taking action requires. We've become conditioned to believe that consuming is equivalent to taking action, often justifying it to ourselves as researching, gaining inspiration, or deepening our knowledge. This passive action isn't moving us toward our goals. The more time we spend consuming, the less time we devote to taking action because, subconsciously, it feels safer to stay stuck exactly where we are.

Our obsession with being a perpetual student and obtaining more certifications often results in a string of alphabet soup behind our name versus tangible results in our business. If consumption alone were the solution, we would all be successful by now.

The endless consumption often serves as an escape from our current reality and clouds our judgment, leading to boredom and unnecessary pivots. The reality is that building a business is far from glamorous, and the Internet has distorted our perception of reality. Building a business involves strategically building a solid foundation by consistently executing basic actions.

Here's an unspoken truth that many industry leaders are unwilling to share: almost every method out there works. The reason you might not be achieving the desired results is the constant switch from one strategy to another, always in pursuit of the elusive quick fix or hidden secret that promises unrealistic results like six figures in six days for novice entrepreneurs. The problem is that we're not allowing any strategy the necessary time needed to yield the results we desire. This desire for instant results ultimately leaves us unsure of what we truly want, leading to frustration when building a business.

The majority of the clients I work with already possess the knowledge needed to build a lucrative business. There's just one thing standing in their way—themselves. Gosh, that hits home a little, doesn't it? However, once you grow tired of the excuses that have been holding you back, you open the door to opportunity. This requires releasing the need for external validation.

The Endless Cycle of External Validation

Social media showcases our addiction to the cycle of external validation. When we create a post and release it into the online space, our immediate focus shifts to the engagement it receives. The influx of likes triggers the release of dopamine in our brains, creating a sense of reward. Each like, comment, share, or engagement provides another hit of dopamine, leading our brains to associate social media usage with positive feelings. This forms a habit loop, compelling us to incessantly check our phones for notifications, as the quest for validation becomes addictive. The worry about the algorithm, the desire to go viral, and the compulsive phone-checking become ingrained habits.

Devoting excessive energy to social media is an exhausting, uphill battle because the exchange of energy is often uneven. We give and give, and the validation may not match the effort invested. Social media has played a role in convincing us that the number of likes and followers directly correlates with business success. Here's a reality check: followers, likes, comments, saves, and shares don't pay the bills, nor do they determine your worth as a human being.

At our core, the desire for acceptance and approval runs deep. This need for acceptance is rooted in our primal instincts, reaching back to our early ancestors. The relentless pursuit of external validation only leads to a sense of lack, creating a void within us. This void can only be filled by one person — ourselves. The answers we seek are already within us. Our task is to be authentic, embracing who we are and not conforming to what the world expects us to be.

Breaking free from the endless cycle of seeking external validation is liberating because it empowers you to control your reactions, engage in activities that excite you, and experience satisfaction and freedom. By not relying on the world for validation, you can pursue what brings you joy and live life on your terms.

Business Strategy Is the Easy Part

Learning the strategic aspects of running a successful business is relatively straightforward, but the unspoken reality—one that many won't openly discuss—is that it's the most significant personal development journey imaginable. Every insecurity, doubt, subconscious belief, and bad habit you possess will be magnified. Ultimately, it becomes a battle between you and yourself. There will be many days when the temptation to quit is strong because setbacks are inevitable. Without holding yourself accountable and maintaining a keen awareness of your self-sabotaging behaviors, the journey becomes an uphill battle. To truly understand why we fall into patterns of self-sabotage, we must uncover the root cause, and often it's because, deep down, we're afraid.

Action Item: Note to Self

Write a letter to yourself dated one year in the future. State the things you have accomplished, the challenges you have overcome, and where you are now because you gave yourself permission.

Chapter 15

Make Fear Your Friend

This four-letter F-word—fear—holds more incredible people back than anything in life. Whether it's fear of failure, fear of judgment, or even fear of success, this emotion is a master of disguise, emerging in different forms as your business grows. It can swiftly become the driving force in your life, using your own fears against you to keep you stuck in the discomfort of the present because you fear the unknown future. Until the discomfort becomes unbearable, you remain stuck; often our minds overvalue security to avoid possible failure.

Fear, in its essence, isn't inherently bad. It's merely an emotion, not an absolute truth. While fear can grab our attention, it often paralyzes us, preventing us from stepping into the highest version of ourselves because we interpret it in the wrong way. Fear will always be present; no matter how hard you try, you can't escape or outrun it. The key is to make fear your ally, leaning into it when it's trying to get your attention instead of letting it become an enemy that holds you back. In order to really understand fear, we need to discuss the three-pound organ behind our eyes . . . a.k.a. the brain.

The Brain

Our brain's primary function is to keep us alive by safeguarding us from danger, and it aims to do so in a way that conserves energy. It is constantly on the lookout for threats to our safety, 24-7. The more safety and predictability it perceives, the less potential risk it senses. Because its role is to keep us alive, our brain seeks to keep us safe by anticipating worst-case scenarios of anything that could potentially go wrong—though often it doesn't. Our brain resists anything uncomfortable or new because it would require additional energy expenditure. This is why much of our lives is spent on autopilot, allowing our brains to conserve energy.

Security and comfort keep us safe, but they can also dim our light. We avoid fear to maintain certainty, and certainty provides a sense of safety. However, when nothing is certain, anything is possible. So, what does this have to do with fear and your ability to build a business? The process of building a business is full of risk and uncertainty, therefore the ability to recognize where fear is holding us back is paramount.

Once upon a time, our brains had to protect us from real dangers, like wild animals that could pose a threat—lions and tigers and bears, oh my! Fortunately, we don't encounter these life-threatening situations regularly. However, the stress of everyday life triggers the same chemical response—known as fight-or flight—in an attempt to keep us safe, though this response can actually suppress our ability to make high-level decisions. This can be utterly exhausting and often leads to burnout. The irony is that we frequently worry about things that won't actually harm us, allowing fear to take the reins.

The brain would rather be sure that it's right instead of being uncertain about a potential outcome as it perceives this as safe, even though you're in pain. It's easy to complain that everything is against us and remain in a reactive mode, overlooking opportunities hiding in plain sight. We become deeply attached to our excuses by adopting a victim mentality and remain stuck in this cycle until the pain becomes unbearable.

The fear we experience often stems from the brain's attempt to protect us from potential future pain, leading to procrastination and avoidance of action. The brain tends to focus on what we don't want, amplifying our limitations and overshadowing our desires. As indicated by a 2018 Yale study, growth occurs in the face of uncertainty, when the brain is challenged to adapt and learn.[7] Embracing change and consistently taking action is essential to rewiring the brain and overcoming its resistance to change. Fear can serve as a guide, pointing toward areas that require attention. Leaning into fear instead of stepping back fosters resilience and facilitates personal and professional development.

When we recognize that life's challenges are prompting us to pay attention and offering valuable lessons, we realize that life is happening for us, not to us. We regain control of

---

7. Bart Massi and Christopher H. Donahue, "Aren't sure? Brain is primed for learning," *YaleNews*, July 19, 2018, https://news.yale.edu/2018/07/19/arent-sure-brain-primed-learning.

the driver's seat and can move fear to the back seat. Pain is inevitable, but the suffering that comes from prolonging the pain is a choice. In having difficult conversations, facing the things we've been avoiding, and confronting our fears head-on, we break free from suffering.

Retrain Your Brain

Our brains are wired for negativity, constantly scanning our environment for threats. Whatever we tell it to search for, it will find. Here's a quick demonstration: Look around the room and count all the green objects you see. Now, try to recall the yellow objects. It's likely you'll struggle to remember the yellow items because your focus was on counting the green ones.

This principle can either work to our advantage as business owners or hinder our progress as a self-fulfilling prophecy that keeps us stuck in our head. If your focus is on obstacles, you'll likely see limitations, similar to noticing the green objects. These perceived limitations then become excuses to sidestep challenging or uncomfortable tasks. However, by shifting your mindset to one of curiosity and asking, "How can I make this work?" you'll start to see opportunities instead of obstacles—much like the yellow objects that were there all along, just not initially in your awareness.

Training the brain to recognize opportunities and take action despite the lack of concrete proof is crucial for personal and professional growth. The brain tends to reinforce existing beliefs, make decisions based on familiar patterns, and seek evidence to support those beliefs. Shifting the focus away from limitations and toward opportunities is a transformative approach that can open up new possibilities.

The process of training your brain to see opportunities and overcome fears and self-limiting beliefs is a gradual one that requires intentional and consistent effort. It takes courage to step out of your comfort zone and take action. Often, fears are rooted in hypothetical scenarios and what-if thinking about situations that haven't occurred.

Recognizing this and actively challenging such thoughts can be a powerful step toward changing your mindset and embracing opportunities. It's about shifting the focus from potential negative outcomes to the positive possibilities that can arise from taking action. Fear should be viewed not as a roadblock but as a catalyst for positive action. This empowers you to achieve what you truly desire. It's a shift from fighting to keep limitations in place to actively pursuing your aspirations.

In the initial stages of building a business, you're fueled by excitement and enthusiasm, driven by the belief that your product or service will positively impact lives. However, as the business evolves, you encounter new and uncomfortable territories that spark thoughts of doubt, worry, and anxiety. Your brain, wired for safety, responds to the unfamiliar by hitting the brakes, leading to a cascade of questioning. At times, you may even contemplate returning to the perceived safety of a 9-to-5 job.

Amid these challenges, it's crucial to make a commitment to yourself and your desired outcome. Take responsibility for your goals, show up consistently, and put in the necessary work to bring your vision to life. The resistance you face isn't a signal you should quit but a sign pointing you in the right direction. I get it—this is HARD—but when you shift your focus to the things you *can* do instead of focusing on what you can't do yet, your life will transform right before your eyes. The negative inner voice loses its influence when you deny it power. Fear and doubt are universal, but don't let them deter you from pursuing the life you desire. Embrace the unfamiliarity of evolution. Your ability to navigate uncertainty will define your success as an entrepreneur.

Train your brain to identify opportunities by posing questions like "How can I make this work?" when confronted with challenges, and you'll uncover new possibilities. The lack of results isn't necessarily a lack of knowledge, but a lack of focus on the opportunities surrounding us. Where your focus goes, your energy flows.

Awareness of the thoughts racing through your head allows you to regain control of the chatter in your brain. By acknowledging these thoughts, questioning them, and working through the resistance that has been keeping you stuck, you can take the next best step forward, no matter how small it may seem. One step leads to another, creating momentum that generates results. It all begins with an awareness of the fear that's holding you back.

Leaning In to Fear

My friend, you're wasting a significant amount of energy avoiding the very things that could transform your life. Energy is one of your most valuable assets. Begin by leaning in to the things that scare you. Over time, they won't be as intimidating. Once you acknowledge your fear, you can take steps to confront it and leverage it to your advantage. I challenge you to push yourself to take action instead of channeling your energy into avoidance. Each small step you take adds to the momentum, gradually breaking down the barriers that have held you back.

One of my favorite illustrations of this concept is the experience of jumping off a diving board. The first time you climb up the ladder, your nerves kick in and your heart starts to race. Doubts flood your mind—what if you forget how to swim? What if you can't find the surface of the water? What if you embarrass yourself and end up belly flopping into the pool? The thought spiral intensifies as you reach the end of the diving board. But somewhere, despite the uncertainty, you decide to impress your friends and take the leap. You jump into the pool, resurface, and swim to the side.

You did it and guess what? It was actually really fun! Encouraged by the thrill, you repeat the process, each time feeling less nervous. Over time, you not only overcome the fear but also learn to perform fancy dives and flips. All because you made the decision to confront the fear and take the plunge.

The tricky aspect of fear is that it triggers the same bodily responses as excitement. Take public speaking, for instance—I used to dread it. Now, I frequently speak on stage. My heart still races, my mouth goes dry, and my palms and armpits sweat excessively. Many would assume that feeling these sensations means they are afraid of public speaking. I have learned to reframe this mindset to realize that it's not fear that I'm experiencing; rather, it's that I'm so darn excited to help empower and educate others to make the life they desire a reality. It's our interpretation of fear that often hinders us, leading to excuses that impede our progress.

It's time to stop making excuses and claim what you want. Excuses are killing your dreams because you're staying in your comfort zone and fighting for your limitations instead of fighting for what you truly desire. Everything in life that you want is on the other side of your fear. It's right outside your comfort zone. It's so much easier to be one step away from a decision than to take a step into the unknown. Discomfort is temporary; stepping into the person you want to become will change not only your life, but the lives of others as well. In order to gain a better understanding of how fear can hold us back, in the next three chapters, we'll look at the three most common worries that hold business owners back.

Action Item: Kick Fear to the Curb

How is fear holding you back from creating the life you desire? How can you release these fears and take action?

Chapter 16

Fear of Failure

Growing up, I allowed fear to control my life, leading me to become an overachiever fueled by external validation. The fear of disappointing others drove me to excel in everything I did. I even managed to graduate, pass state boards, and obtain my license before I could legally drink. The educational system had instilled in me a fear of failure, portraying it as the worst possible outcome. Coupled with a career where mistakes could have serious consequences, the fear of failure ran deep through my veins.

This self-imposed narrative I created, viewing failure as a direct reflection of my worth, granted fear far too much power over my life for far too long. Thankfully, I have developed the self-awareness to acknowledge and release the choke hold that fear had on me. I've come to realize that failure is merely feedback and, in retrospect, I realize my failures have taught me more than all of my successes combined.

Embracing Failure

In our relentless pursuit of success, the fear of failure often looms at the forefront of our minds. What if, however, we could give ourselves permission to fail and transform failure into a catalyst for growth? Leaning in to fear emerges as a more productive use of our time and energy than avoiding the challenges that scare us because we might fail. The willingness to make mistakes, and learn from them, becomes a powerful accelerator for personal and professional growth.

Consider professional athletes as a prime example. They encounter failure constantly, but they use it as an opportunity to adjust, adapt, and improve their approach. In baseball, professional players strike out more often than they hit home runs. Basketball players miss more than half of their shots during game play, and professional soccer players miss, on average, 75 percent of their shots. We can learn a valuable lesson from these athletes in that failure is simply information which can guide us toward the success hidden on the other side.

No one is immune to failure, but your willingness to try, even if you make mistakes along the way, will help you grow. Even if you fail, you are still much further ahead than those who weren't even willing to try. Therefore, the sooner you accept that fear will always be present, the quicker you will reach your goals because mistakes provide valuable feedback we need to stay on track. It's crucial to recognize that making mistakes doesn't erase the progress you've made. Failure doesn't truly exist unless you stop trying and do nothing. You've handled every setback until this point.

Failure doesn't mean that success isn't possible; rather, it's a concept we've created in our minds to let ourselves off the hook and quit. In reality, failure builds resilience. Often, we let the fear of failure paralyze us, preventing us from even starting because achieving those big, intimidating dreams feels impossible or we doubt we're worthy of the life we desire. This couldn't be further from the truth. Failing means you're doing what others won't—taking action and trying new things.

What matters most is what you do after something you try doesn't work. What lessons can you learn? When you realize that failures are lessons in disguise, opportunities reveal themselves. You're retraining your brain, and this process takes practice—lots of it. The more you practice this new skill, the easier it gets because you're learning to bounce back even stronger.

You are worthy of the dream that has been placed on your heart. If you're willing to accept failures along the way, you can make that dream a reality. Stop letting the fear of failure hinder the impact you are meant to make on this world.

Learn to Be a Beginner

When was the last time you were a beginner? Many of us find it challenging to pinpoint such a moment because being a beginner is often uncomfortable. In the initial stages of learning something new, we're usually not very good at it. I can vividly recall my first group ski lesson—I slid into a ditch and spent the entire time struggling to get my boot back into the ski binding because I was too stubborn to ask for help. Had I admitted that I had no clue what I was doing and embraced being a beginner, I wouldn't have missed out on almost the entire lesson.

Being a beginner can be fun because it allows us to play and teaches our brain that failure isn't a bad thing—it's just practice. Think about how many times you fell when learning how to ride a bike. No one expected you to get it on the first try, so you kept practicing and getting better. Being a beginner at something is an opportunity to learn, play, grow, change, and get better! As a beginner, there's often less judgment, creating a space for exploration.

The real learning happens in doing, in taking action. You'll never feel fully ready to ride the bike. You have to learn to make small adjustments so your body stays balanced, coordinate speed while pedaling, and brake without launching over the handlebars. It's in the willingness to be a beginner again that you truly grow and learn. You may fall down multiple times, but you keep getting back up because you are committed to the outcome of being able to ride a bike. The more you practice, the better you get, and you may even find yourself riding with one hand, popping wheelies, or, dare I say, completely letting go of the handlebars?

We often overlook a fundamental truth: mastery in any skill requires practice, and improvement stems from taking actionable steps. The more attempts you make, the more insights you gain. I'm still navigating my way through fully embracing this concept. This is exactly why I committed to recording over 225 podcast episodes last year. Recognizing that reps get results, I understood that to improve my skill set,

I had to put in the work. Today, my podcast stands as one of the most significant lead generation sources in my business, all because I embraced the role of a beginner. Reflecting on the inaugural episode from 2022 still makes me cringe, yet it also instills a sense of pride in acknowledging the considerable progress I've made.

The practice of doing new things leads to more knowledge while improving your skills and giving you valuable experience. You have to make the decision, commit to it, and stop fighting harder for your limitations than you do for your dreams. Your life is YOUR responsibility. The hardest part about change and doing something new is that, at first, you're going to suck, and no one likes the feeling of not being good at something. Your first attempt at anything will likely be subpar, but you can't reach your hundredth without your first. Building a business follows a similar trajectory; true proficiency comes from applying our knowledge in practical situations.

Expecting yourself not to fail is like expecting a baby to stop trying to learn to walk after their first fall. Falling is inevitable, but engaging in activities that you might not be good at without some practice is a fundamental step toward your goals. It provides the opportunities to learn, adapt, and adjust, ultimately moving you forward. Setbacks are merely a test of your resilience, and it's essential to grant yourself permission to make mistakes.

Let's welcome the chaos and embrace the journey. This moment is the only certainty we have, so use it to start. Start scared, start as a beginner—just start. Refuse to settle for a mediocre life.

Going After the Life You Want

No matter who you are, every journey begins at ground zero. It's a choice between pursuing the life you desire or settling for the one you're handed. Never settle. The decision to be ready is in your hands—a commitment to stop settling, take a chance, and reclaim control. Be resistant to the discouraging voice inside your mind that says "you can't," and amplify the whisper that insists "you can." Recognize your potential impact on the world, for playing small doesn't serve you or anyone else.

The power lies in making decisions; deciding to take action despite the looming fear is pivotal. Decisions propel us toward our goals, unveiling opportunities right in front of us. Our default brain wiring leans toward negativity, designed to safeguard us by demanding attention. Shifting our perspective from the fear of failure to focus on what could go right alters our outlook and is critical to achieving the results we desire. Undoubtedly, judgments—both positive and negative—await us, but we get to decide whether succumbing to them leads to a life filled with regrets. Thriving necessitates a willingness to face failure, either to navigate through challenges or to decide that a particular path may not be our calling.

Success isn't born from merely doing things; it's about doing the right things. If you persist in doing the wrong things, increasing your efforts won't boost your chances of success; it will only expedite your failure. Successful individuals embrace actions that others shy away from, often living beyond the confines of their comfort zones. Here's the uncomplicated formula for success: double your rate of failure. Contrary to perceiving failure as the adversary of success, consider it a valuable teacher. Learn from your mistakes and make as many as you can, for it is on the other side of failure that success awaits.

Keep in mind, faith and fear both demand belief in the unseen. Channel the faith in yourself instead of surrendering to the recurrent fear. Your reluctance to face failure holds you back from seizing incredible opportunities. The what-if scenarios, now treated as certainties without evidence, are holding you back. Acknowledge them, then usher them to the back seat— they're slowing you down. This journey is yours, and you're at the wheel. Focus on potential gains, not losses. Imagine a life where failure is off the table. Beliefs are like thought habits; limiting beliefs shape the lens through which you view your life. Successful individuals challenge these limitations, while unsuccessful ones incessantly try to validate them. Quit dodging failure—embrace it and make it your ally.

Perfectionism

Reflecting on my own experiences, I recognize that I allowed excuses and a craving for certainty to slow my progress. Waiting until you have everything figured out is a hindrance. Fear of the unknown and the imagined consequences often hold us captive. We concoct potential outcomes to stay within our comfort zones, becoming reactive instead of proactive. These self-created narratives, born out of a need for protection, hinder our growth.

Most fears are intellectual, not physical threats like lions and tigers. The risk of actual harm or danger is minimal.

Perfectionism often leads to procrastination and indecisiveness because we're craving certainty, an attempt by our brain to keep us safe. The unfortunate reality is that perfectionist tendencies can cause us to create unrealistic standards and expectations for ourselves. We want to know exactly how things are going to play out before they happen. However, when we are so worried about the future, we miss the joy of the present moment. This holds us back from even starting and becomes a stumbling block in our journey toward success. It's important to get curious and figure out which behaviors are blocking your progress toward your goals so that you don't end up sabotaging your efforts.

The fear of failure emerges from a sense of inadequacy, preventing you from initiating tasks in order to avoid potential pain. To break free from this cycle, you must act, even in the face of uncertainty. Recognize the gap between your current self and your desired self, let go of the need for constant validation, and embrace the journey of personal growth.

Recall a moment in your life when you experienced an event that, while exciting, was new. It could be buying your first house, adopting a pet, or having a child. Chances are you felt unprepared and uncertain. Despite the nerves and lack of complete knowledge, you stepped up, did your best with what you had, learned, adjusted, and didn't let fear hinder you. This experience serves as a reminder that the fears in your mind aren't necessarily true.

Action Item: Then What?

This exercise is based on the work of Dr. Jordan Peterson, author of *12 Rules for Life*.

Many of our fears are either unlikely to happen or are not based in reality. The thought spiral, however, can hold us back and magnify our fears. The key is to start questioning your fears to regain control. It may look something like this:

I am afraid to quit my job.

Why?

Because what if my business fails?

Then what?

I will be embarrassed.

Then what?

I will need to go find another job.

Then what?

I'll be right back at ground zero.

Then what?

I can find another way to make money.

Chapter 17

Fear of Judgment

In life, judgment is inevitable—both positive and negative. Are you letting the judgment of others slow down your success? What if, instead of being weighed down by the opinions of others, we could rise above and navigate our journey with confidence? In a world filled with uncertainties, there is one constant: some people are not going to understand you, and that's perfectly okay!

Do not allow others' opinions to dictate your path or hinder your progress. It's important to recognize that others' opinions of you are projections of their reality, not rooted in fact. You can't control what other people do or say, but you can control how you let these judgments impact you. Often, we create a story about what others think of us, creating unnecessary assumptions and leading to feelings of rejection and disappointment. Despite your fears, focus on serving others and the impact you can make. Understand that being misunderstood by a few is a small price to pay for impacting many.

Embrace the reality that doubters, mean-spirited individuals, naysayers, and Internet trolls will always exist. Ask yourself:

does this person's opinion and judgment really matter? Why are you valuing their opinion when they don't even know you? Confidence is quiet, and insecurity is loud—often, it's those sitting on the sidelines who judge the loudest. But do others' opinions pay your bills? No! Channel your inner Elsa and let it go.

Life is too short to waste your two most valuable assets— time and energy—on things that don't truly matter. Be unapologetically you. It's okay that not everyone will agree with you or understand your journey. Stop giving your power away by playing small to avoid being judged by others.

Even the act of writing this book has brought up the fear of judgment. What will people think? What if they don't like what I have to say? What if I spend all this time writing a book and no one buys it? In acknowledging these thoughts and shifting my focus from self-doubt to the impact I will have on others, I begin to transform fear into a catalyst for positive change. I start to ask myself questions like: How can my story help others? How can it empower someone else to pursue the dream on their heart? What bigger impact can I create? What if it all works out?

Stop holding back your authentic self because you're afraid of what others will think. It's time to stop chasing and start attracting by showing up as yourself. You won't be for everyone and that's a good thing! Lean into your people—those who appreciate, value, and accept you as you are.

What you think of yourself is what truly matters, not the opinions of others. Those spending time and energy judging you aren't your people—they feel insecure, and their lack of confidence leads them to judge others. Releasing the fear of judgment allows for faster growth. If you are willing to get out of your own way, you will change your life and help others change theirs. Reflect on how you are showing up. Are you speaking your mind? And my personal favorite from Lindsey Schwartz, founder of Powerhouse Women, "Are you willing to be misunderstood by a few so you can impact many?"

At the end of the day, most people aren't paying as much attention to us as we believe. The ego, fearing rejection, often leads us to overestimate the attention we receive. The only opinion that truly matters is yours.

So how do we move past the deeply ingrained fear of judgment? Shift the focus outward on how you can serve others and on the impact you will make. You do not need anyone else's permission to go after the life you desire— just your own. Give yourself permission: permission to try, permission to fail, permission to learn, permission to grow, and permission to keep promises to yourself. Detaching from the outcome relieves the pressure and allows us to focus on serving others rather than on self-centered concerns.

Comparison, the thief of joy, is exhausting. We are often so preoccupied with what everyone else is doing that we forget what we truly want. Excessive energy spent on comparing ourselves to others distracts us and holds us back from embodying our authentic selves. Comparing ourselves to everyone else usually happens in areas where we feel insecure.

Stepping out of your comfort zone and doing new things may create resistance, as your brain is wired to keep you safe. Your brain is rewiring itself, and this process takes time. Accept that it's part of the journey and lean in to it.

Action Item: Releasing the Fear of Judgment

Take a moment and get quiet. Close your eyes and become aware of the feelings of judgment that you may have buried deep within. Acknowledge your feelings and then when you are ready, write down these fears. Once you have taken the time to do this, tear apart the paper releasing the fear of judgment and thereby giving yourself permission to fully accept and embrace yourself just as you are.

Chapter 18

Fear of Success

The fear of success may be the most common, yet overlooked, fear that holds us back from living the life we desire. Often, fear of success will manifest as self-sabotage, which goes hand in hand with its bestie, procrastination. If you don't have massive self-awareness, this leaves you wondering why you aren't making the progress you say that you want.

This fear runs on a subconscious narrative about the potential costs of achieving the success we say we desire because success often brings new challenges and responsibilities. Our desire for comfort leads us to prefer the familiarity of our current situation, even if it's not ideal, over the uncertainty that success may bring. For example, if you're a mom, success might imply more time away from family, raising questions about your ability to handle increased workloads. This fear prompts thoughts like; *If I can barely manage now, how will I cope with the success I desire?* or *Will achieving financial freedom change how others perceive me?* These thoughts about the potential new challenges and responsibilities of future success directly feed into our fears of judgment and failure and can be paralyzing.

198 | The CEO Method
198 | The CEO Method

Thoughts like this are real and show up in sneaky ways. For example, it might be making excuses as to why you couldn't show up on social media, or it may be missing deadlines. Perhaps you don't follow up with clients or ask for a referral, because you don't want to be a "bother." It's avoiding looking at your business banking and missing invoices and payments. These behaviors are holding you back.

You know exactly what it is you need to do, but you are too fearful to do it. When you take the time to unpack these fears, you begin to regain control. Fear will always be there no matter the level of success you achieve, but gaining control of the fear is key. When you take the time to dismantle these underlying thoughts and beliefs by questioning their validity, you begin to regain control. All too often, the only person between you and the life you desire is you.

Success brings an unknown set of challenges, and since our brain is working so hard to keep us safe, we would rather stay stuck and avoid the disappointment that will result if things don't work out. We may even fear that achieving a certain level of the success we desire will change certain relationships or require us to let go of relationships that we know no longer serve us. We aren't willing, however, to have these hard conversations that would allow us to move forward.

Another form of procrastination is running away from your fears by constantly distracting yourself in a cycle of overconsumption. Have you ever taken another course instead of implementing everything you learned in the last course you took because you thought you needed more knowledge before you could take action?

Overconsumption sets us up for disappointment because it creates unrealistic expectations and decreases our creativity. It's the breeding ground for impostor syndrome because we have created a false reality based on someone else's highlight reel. And it won't help you make any progress toward making your dreams a reality.

We would rather stay in our comfort zone, where we know we're safe, than risk disappointing someone. We get stuck here. We know what will move the business forward but aren't willing to do those things. When you accept that uncertainty will always be there, you can acknowledge it and reframe it as a catalyst for growth instead of something that stops us in our tracks.

Being trapped by fear keeps us focused on ourselves rather than on how we can get out of our own way and start serving others. You have to do the scary stuff to get the results you desire. The degree to which you can handle uncertainty dictates your degree of success. Fear of success means that you are afraid to take full responsibility for your life. It's time to stop blaming others, playing the victim, making excuses, and hiding your authenticity. It's time to be vulnerable and willing to put yourself out there. It's time to feel the fear and do it anyway!

When you finally acknowledge and release your fears, you break through the stories holding you back and begin to step into the life you're meant to live. Remember, discomfort is a sign that you're growing. Yes, your life will change as you evolve, but what if you shift your thinking to a perspective of hope and optimism? Keep in mind the possibilities that will come with success, and keep in mind that, as Marie Forleo says, "everything is figureoutable." We're meant to evolve as humans, but when we set unrealistic expectations, we slow down our ability to make progress.

I am a recovering people pleaser through and through. I think it's a combination of the enneagram type nine in me and a life fueled by external validation. I'm still working on it. I knew years before I left my 9-to-5 career that I needed to make a change, but there was one thing stopping me. It wasn't the money, it wasn't fear of failure—it was a sense of guilt.

I had my dream job working in an outpatient orthopedic physical therapy clinic. I had worked my butt off and graduated from college so I could have a license on the wall telling me I was qualified. Who was I to want more out of life? Who was I to walk away from what I always said I wanted? Who was I to take a leap that logically didn't make sense?

I stopped and realized that the 16 years of working as a therapist weren't wasted. In fact, they were preparing me and giving me critical experience for the role I currently hold. I spent those 16 years empowering and educating over 50,000 patients . . . yes, I did the math. I helped them through the lowest points in their recovery and celebrated every milestone along the way to achieving their final goal. Now I get to do what I loved about this career every single day but in an even bigger capacity. I get to empower and educate my clients to achieve the financial success that they desire. It's what I loved about my career. Seeing the transformation. Uncovering the potential within my clients to create a life full of freedom and flexibility.

Please know that it's okay to be grateful for what you have but to never stop working for what you want. As you evolve as a person, your career may evolve. You are on this earth for a purpose, and your job is to figure out what that purpose is. It's not a pretty process and involves a lot of trial and error; however, when you are willing to take action and fail along the way, opportunities have a magical way of presenting themselves. The crazy part is, they were there the whole time; you were just too focused on your fears to see them.

Action Item: Facing Your Fear

It's time to get really honest with yourself. What is your biggest fear? List the benefits you get from staying stuck in this cycle of fear. What don't you have to do? What conversations can you avoid? What identity can you hold on to?

Chapter 19

Information + Implementation = Results

This book has given you the step-by-step framework to build a profitable business that supports the life you desire. However, all the knowledge in the world won't create the results you want until you give yourself permission to step out of your comfort zone and take action. This, my friend, is the secret that you have been searching for in every course, in every freebie you download, and in every mentor that you invest in. Implementation is the missing piece to achieving the results you desire. The good news is that to get the results you want, all you have to do is get out of your own way and put in the work. The bad news? No one is going to do it for you.

If you knew that taking action would get you the results you desire, would you be willing to do the work? How willing would you be to show up on the days you didn't feel like it? How willing would you be to get uncomfortable and face the fears that have held you back for so long? It starts with making the decision to keep the small promises you make to yourself and not quitting at the first bit of resistance that pops up. Every action in life either gives us the result we want or the lesson we need. At the end of the day, a lack of action leads to a lack of results. You can have the best idea in the world, but if you're not taking action, you will never create the reality you desire.

The people who you hold in high regard and deem as successful are no different from you. They aren't smarter or more qualified than you. They don't have a secret code, and most of them didn't just wake up millionaires. The only difference is that they made a decision to push excuses and self-limiting beliefs aside, gave themselves permission to fail, and showed up and took action every single day. They detached from the outcome and embraced the journey while using data to drive their decisions. And they kept in mind that their successes and failures were not an indicator of their inherent worth as a human being.

All too often, we miss incredible opportunities because we neglect to act on our amazing ideas, and we don't implement the tasks that would move us toward our goals. How many times have you had an idea for a product or service only to see it on store shelves a year or two later? Funny story: I remember sitting in the pediatrician's office for the first time with my oldest. There was a basket of books on the counter, and I began flipping through them. The titles of these children's books were hysterical, and I wondered that if other people could sell books with these absurd titles, maybe I could too. I had an idea for a book with the title *Pigs with Wigs*. I said this as a joke; however, two years later, while at my sister-in-law's house, I saw a book in my niece's collection titled—you guessed it—*Pigs with Wigs*, copyright date a year after I sat in the pediatrician's office. Someone wrote the book and was now making money off it because they took action to bring this idea to life, whereas I didn't.

How many incredible ideas that could change lives have died in the notes app of your phone or in a journal because you didn't have the courage to pursue it? We often allow the "how" to hold us back. We're afraid to take messy action, but every single great creation began as something that seemed impossible—a crazy idea—because it hadn't been done before. While that children's book probably wouldn't have impacted others' lives, maybe it could have changed my life.

Success usually doesn't come from the big events; it's an accumulation of micro-actions we take every single day. If you aim for the slightest bit of improvement daily by taking the next best step forward, imagine where you will be in a month, a year, five years from now. Your life could look completely different in the best way. Therefore, make the question not *if* you will succeed, but *when* you succeed, and how big that success will be.

Simple tasks are often overshadowed by excuses for three reasons: they are easy to put off, results aren't immediate, and they seem insignificant. However, these seemingly small actions are significant. Building a business is a long game, and it's important to remember that your pace does not have to look like anyone else's. The key is to find a consistent rhythm that is sustainable for you based on the season of life you are currently in. There will be ups and downs, twists and turns. Believe that you can, believe that you will, and then take massive action to get it done. There will always be others ahead of you, and there will always be people behind you, but nothing will happen until you take action.

Breaking the Procrastination Cycle

The hardest part of taking action is overcoming the initial mental resistance to getting started. We get in our heads, we play out a million and one potential outcomes, we overanalyze, and by the time we think we're ready, we're exhausted because we've used all our energy playing out imaginary situations and negotiating with ourselves. Procrastination is a protective mechanism designed to keep us in our comfortable current circumstances rather than risk the unknown.

In order to break through these comfortable current circumstances, action is required. Action is what will create proof for your brain to see that it is possible to achieve the success you desire. The longer you delay action, the harder it will be because your brain doesn't think it is important to you. You will go back into fight-or-flight mode because you've added another level of resistance.

In order to make progress toward your goals, massive self-awareness is key to identifying what self-sabotaging behaviors are holding you back. Once you identify the roadblock, the way to get unstuck is by taking action. This isn't always easy. Often, we've created big mountains out of molehills because of the sheer magnitude of energy we tell ourselves it will take to achieve our goals.

A simple yet effective way to combat the procrastination cycle is to break the thought train by using the five second rule coined by Mel Robbins.[8] This simple exercise has helped me to stop dwelling in procrastination, always putting things off, by eliminating my initial resistance. It's easy. When you find yourself tempted to put something off, count down from five to zero, then immediately take action. For example, in the morning when your alarm goes off and you find yourself hitting the snooze button because your warm, cozy bed is much more comfortable than getting yourself up and taking on the day. The next time you hear your alarm go off, count down 5-4-3-2-1 and take action. The resistance we face is a test of your commitment, and overcoming it builds resilience to equip you for the next stage of the journey.

You will never get to where you want to go unless you take action. No matter how much you consume, true learning only occurs when you actually do something. Let's consider riding a bike as an example. You could watch people ride bikes, study the techniques they use, read all the books on cycling, but if you think you can consume all this information and hop on a bike without falling, you're in for a surprise.

Action creates more clarity because it gives you more information as to what is working and what's not. What feels aligned and what no longer serves you. If we're constantly barreling down the highway and ignoring the flashing light next to the fuel gauge on our dashboard, we will run out of gas.

_____

8. Mel Robbins, *The 5 Second Rule* (Brentwood, TN: Savio Republic, 2017).

Ready Is a Decision

In our lives, we have far more choices than we realize.

To create or consume.

To compare or create.

To compete or collaborate.

To make the choice to make a change because if nothing changes, nothing changes.

Doing the same thing over and over and expecting different results is the definition of insanity. Make the decision to go after the life you want because it's waiting for you on the other side of fear and indecision. Ready is a decision, not a feeling. The only person who can give up on you or label you as a failure is you. The only person who can choose to wake up every single day and put in the work is you. You have control over your actions, reactions, and mindset. Be the person with results, not excuses.

All too often, we complain about things we can change but are afraid to. Stop complaining about the things you haven't taken steps to change, and spend your time taking action to create the change you desire. This may involve short-term sacrifices, but these temporary sacrifices often yield long-term gains. Most of the time, the opportunity is there, but we're afraid to take the risk that accompanies the action. Results happen over time, not overnight.

When you really want something, you will find a way because your self-imposed excuses are no longer bigger than what you desire. Here's a perfect example to demonstrate this point. I remember when I was a freshman in high school and Doc Martens were the "in" thing. I wanted this hideous pair of shoes to wear to school with my plaid uniform skirt and button up shirt, but my parents told me there was no way they were dropping over $100 for a pair of shoes. This was the '90s and $100 was a ton of money. As a 15-year-old, I had no money, but because I wanted these shoes badly enough, I found a way to make enough money to buy them.

Make the Choice

You are in control of your life—and this might sting a little— but being stuck is a choice and being overwhelmed is an excuse. We avoid taking action by deprioritizing the things that would actually move the needle because it's easier to complain and procrastinate than to do what we need to do. Here's the reality: where you end up a year from now is a reflection of the choices you make today. Deciding is the first step to getting everything you desire. Stop waiting for things to change.

If you're not happy with your current circumstances, what are you doing to change your current reality? If you can't change your circumstances, how can you reframe your attitude? You can't change the things that have happened in the past; your power lies in how you respond and what you choose to do in the present.

There is always a next step you can take to change the trajectory of your life. You don't need to have it all figured out; the only thing you need to know is the next best step. Trust that you will figure it out as you go. This is how you will grow your business and achieve the success you desire.

Overthinking and Overwhelm

Overthinking wastes a ton of one of your most valuable assets, energy, and can quickly lead to feelings of overwhelm. When you commit to taking action instead of overthinking, you will make far more progress. You have the ability to adjust as you go and gain valuable insights and data as to what is working and what you can refine. At the end of the day, the level of success you achieve is dictated by your ability to withstand discomfort and resistance.

The next time you find yourself overthinking or overwhelmed, take the time to pause and identify what is causing you to feel that way. When we feel overwhelmed, we don't know where to start, but often there is a solution right in front of us. Take the time to identify the issue in order to solve the problem. One of the fastest ways to decrease the overwhelm is to take a few slow, deep breaths. Breathing is the first thing that changes any time we experience an emotion; by shifting your awareness to the breath, you regain control. Overwhelm is a feeling we choose, and when we take the time to get curious and explore what is at the core of this feeling, we can find the resources to regain control.

Next, list three actions you could take to move forward. These don't have to be monumental tasks. Choose simple action steps like sending the email you have been putting off, purchasing the mic that's been sitting in your cart for a year, or making a scary ask. Change doesn't demand perfection; it demands we show up and take bold action to get the results we desire. Taking action will help alleviate some of the anxiety and overwhelm and create more momentum. It's physics! But the longer you sit in indecision, the more potential opportunities you miss. Changing your life is your responsibility, and you will often feel like you can't . . . until you learn that you can.

Action Item: Take Action!

Action takers are moneymakers, therefore in order to achieve the results you want, you need to take action. Use the following questions to help you get started.

What do I need to do this week?

What worked well last week that I can do again this week?

What didn't work well last week and what can I learn from it?

Am I on track to reach my goals? If so, I'll take the opportunity to celebrate. If not, why? What is holding me back?

Conclusion

Your Permission Slip

"Life moves pretty fast. If you don't stop and look around once in a while, you could miss it." Matthew Broderick, *Ferris Bueller's Day Off*

Building a business is an adventure full of opportunities, surprises, and unexpected twists and turns. It's like taking the most epic road trip of your life. Before embarking on your journey, you need to do some planning to prepare for the trip ahead. In order to reach your goals, you need to clarify exactly where you are and where you want to go. Get yourself ready, put your destination in your GPS, and tell fear to hop in the back seat because you are the driver.

As you start your journey, take a moment to defrost your windows, ensuring a clear view of the road ahead. Along the way, pay attention to your car's warning lights, refuel regularly, and navigate the occasional detours that will come your way. Sometimes, you'll need to switch on your lights to navigate through darkness or recalculate your route after a wrong turn. Expect bumps, slow zones, and the occasional setback, like a flat tire that threatens to ruin your day—unless you decide otherwise.

The process of growing a business can feel lonely; however, you are not meant to do this alone. Along the journey, you'll encounter amazing individuals willing to keep you company and offering guidance and support to help you navigate the route. It's a wild ride, so take a moment to glance in your rearview mirror, appreciating the progress you've made and paying attention to the signs along the way. The road may be unpredictable, with twists and turns, but when you embrace the journey and stay focused on your destination, you'll find joy in the ride and make the experience a delightful one.

I've provided you with the road map, but the decision to take action is in your hands. Dedicate time to do the work and get the results you desire.

Will it be easy? No.

Will it be worth it? YES!

Stop Waiting

You have the solution to someone's problem. It's time to get out of your own way, check your ego, and share it with the world. We need you! When you fully step into the role of CEO, you take ownership of your life, your business, and the success you achieve. You have made a commitment to yourself to stop making excuses and push through the fear and uncertainty.

You are the CEO of your life and your business. Creating a life that you love comes down to making a decision to get in the game. Take personal responsibility to stop making the excuses that are keeping you small and to start taking action. Make a commitment to yourself, and do what you said you were going to do. You have the power to change your life.

At the end of the day, it's up to you to make the choice to push through the fear and go after the life you want. What's amazing is that success only comes down to one thing—your decision to keep going until you reach the goal you set. An excuse is a challenge you have decided has power over you. If you're serious about changing your life, you'll find a way past your obstacles. If you're not truly committed, you'll find an excuse.

You can't rely on others to push you out of your comfort zone. It's up to you and it starts with a decision. You have total control whether you realize it or not. Your reality is a result of the decisions you have made. Yes, crappy circumstances happen, but you can control how you respond to those circumstances. You get to choose. It's time to take responsibility for yourself and your life. When we stop playing the blame game, we realize that we can paint our own reality. We can rewrite the story we have been living if we don't like how it's going. You always have a choice. Choose the path that is right for you.

You will make mistakes. Things won't always work out like you hoped they would. You'll fall down so many times along the way, but you'll keep getting up as many times as you need to. You have made a decision, so commit to making it happen and stop overthinking. It will all work out. Either you'll succeed or you'll learn another lesson along the way. No one will fight the fight for you or put in the work it takes to get the results you desire.

You have to be the person to make the choice to make a change and then keep the promise you made to yourself. Stop waiting for permission from someone else. While you are playing small, there are others out there not able to step into the version of themselves that they are meant to be. There's a ripple effect that occurs when you step into your purpose. All of the power lies within you. You have the ability to change your life and the lives of others. The life you desire is out there waiting for you to claim it. It's time to get out there and make the money you want so that you can create the impact you desire!

Acknowledgments

How do I even begin to put into words how grateful I am to each and every person that has helped me on my journey? I am humbled by the outpouring of support I have received, and I couldn't have done any of it alone.

Thank you to my husband for believing in me on the days when I didn't. I love the life that we're building together. I can't believe this is real life!

Thank you to my girls. You are my why. I'm here to show you that it's okay to change your mind. If you're not happy, make the choice to make a change. The only permission you need in this world is your own. Live life on your terms, not the terms society has created for you.

Thank you to everyone who gave me a copy of Jake Kelfer's book, *Big Idea to Bestseller*, which was the catalyst for this book. After receiving copies from three separate people, I figured it was time to stop ignoring the nudge and write the book.

Thank you to all of my loyal podcast listeners. You keep me going!

Thank you to my online business besties, especially my life coach, Lauren Marks. You were truly a catalyst for growth, and you truly changed my life.

Thank you to my podcast mentor, JoAnne Bolt. You have completely revolutionized my business by teaching me how to leverage my podcast to grow my business.

Thank you to my copy editor, Catt Editing, and my phenomenal brand photographer, Maddy Sharp.

Thank YOU for reading this book! It still seems completely surreal to call myself an author. Use this book as proof that you have the ability to create the success you desire. YOU have the solution to someone's problem. Get out there and take action!

Recommended Reading

Reading is one of my favorite things to do. Below, you will find a list of business and personal development books that have changed my life. Enjoy!

Atomic Habits by James Clear

Thinking Like a Boss by Kate Crocco

On Purpose by Tanya Dalton

Everything Is Figureoutable by Marie Forleo

Be Your Future Self Now by Dr. Benjamin Hardy

Think and Grow Rich by Napoleon Hill

Fear Is My Homeboy by Judi Holler

The Greatness Mindset by Lewis Howes

Winging It by Emma Isaacs

The One Thing by Gary Keller

Building a StoryBrand by Donald Miller

The High 5 Habit by Mel Robbins

You Are a Badass by Jen Sincero

Don't Forget!

Grab Your Free Resources by visiting **amytraugh.com/ceobook**

And check out our globally ranked podcast, The Motivated CEO, available at **amytraugh.com/podcast** and on all streaming platforms!

About the Author

A self-proclaimed chaos coordinator, Amy Traugh is a three-time business founder, a business strategist specializing in helping women entrepreneurs grow their companies, and the host of The Motivated CEO Podcast.

Through her signature CEO Method, Amy has helped hundreds of online service providers generate the consistent sales they want so they can create the impact they desire without sacrificing their two most valuable assets, time and energy. She is passionate about empowering and educating others how to regain control and design a business built around their lives.

A native of Northeast Ohio, Amy loves escaping to the beach, curling up with a good book, and making memories with her husband and kiddos.

Are you ready to break through your sales plateau and generate more CONSISTENT sales?

Learn more at **amytraugh.com**

www.ingramcontent.com/pod-product-compliance
Lightning Source LLC
Chambersburg PA
CBHW071557210326
41597CB00019B/3287